Open Water Swimming

A Complete Guide for Swimmers and Triathletes

Open Water Swimming

A Complete Guide for Swimmers and Triathletes

EMMA DAVIS

THE CROWOOD PRESS

First published in 2013 by
The Crowood Press Ltd
Ramsbury, Marlborough
Wiltshire SN8 2HR

www.crowood.com

British Library Cataloguing-in-Publication Data
A catalogue record for this book is available from the British Library.

ISBN 978 1 84797 609 3

Typeset by Jean Cussons Typesetting, Diss, Norfolk

Printed and bound in India by Replika Press Pvt Ltd

CONTENTS

Acknowledgements 6

1 Introduction to Open Water Swimming 7

2 Equipment and Getting Started 9

3 Open Water Acclimatization 16

4 Situations to Avoid 23

5 Sighting 29

6 Competitive Open Water Swimming 33

7 Swim Drafting 38

8 Starts, Exits and Turning around Buoys 41

9 Nutrition 52

10 Basic Training Programmes 56

11 Possible Injuries and their Management 70

12 Frequently Asked Questions 81

13 The Final Word 86

Glossary 87

Further Information 92

Index 93

ACKNOWLEDGEMENTS

There are many people without whom this book would not have been written, and I would like to take this opportunity to express my thanks to as many of them as possible. First of all, thank you to my amazing friend and photographer Kirsty Nethercott, my swimming and rehabilitation models Matthew Langston and Luke Francis, computer expert Alex Todd for his help with the anatomical body diagrams, to my two very special proof readers, Ann and Phil, who never tired of re-reading, and to all those at Hampton Pool, Open Water Swim and Liquid Leisure.

CHAPTER 1

INTRODUCTION TO OPEN WATER SWIMMING

Quite simply, open water swimming is swimming in open water: that is, swimming outside in lakes, rivers, canals, reservoirs or the sea. For those who are adrenalin junkies, open water swimming can encompass so-called 'extreme swimming', the riskiest and potentially the most dangerous form of swimming there is.

The History of Open Water Swimming

Open water swimming as a sport dates back to 1810 when Lord Byron swam from Europe to Asia across the Hellespont, or the Dardanelles as we now call it. At the first modern Olympic Games in 1896 the swimming event was held in open water, but as the participating nations became wealthier and more sophisticated, the number of public swimming pools gradually increased, and so it became customary to swim in a pool. This was mirrored in the events of the Olympic Games, as the open water swimming event was eventually replaced by pool swimming, and the number of events proliferated.

But we have moved full circle, because at the Sydney Olympic Games in the year 2000 the triathlon made its first appearance, an event involving a 1,500m swim in Sydney harbour; and in 2008 at the Beijing Olympic Games, open water swimming was back as a competition in its own right, as a 10km race. The General FINA World Championships now include 5, 10 and 25km open water swims, and open water swimming is currently experiencing a real explosion in both mass participation and performance level competition.

We will now explore some of the reasons why you should follow suit and take up open water swimming.

The Benefits of Open Water Swimming

The most important reason for taking up open water swimming, as with any sport, is for pure enjoyment. The feeling of being suspended is so special: in the water your body feels lighter, more elegant and free – it is a whole other world. In the water most of our senses are greatly restricted – eyesight is blurred, hearing is minimal, and there isn't anything to smell or taste – and because of this, the one sense that we have left, touch, is heightened. Thus in the water we feel everything to a much greater degree: the way the water pushes back on our hand and arm as we pull ourselves through it; how the hairs on our legs restrict its flow; the splash of it on our face; even the nastiness of it going up our nose. This is one of the few situations where you are able to experience the sense of touch to such an extent.

Swimming indoors is pleasure enough, but why not head outside to nature? No more the boredom of swimming up and down the pool, endlessly counting the number of lengths you have swum; and also no more all the nasty chemicals required to keep the swimming pool fresh and sanitary – you no longer smell of chlorine for days after you swim, the air is fresh and clean, and there is so much to see! Why stare at a black line when you could be following a ghost carp or even swimming alongside a dolphin?

Swimming is also one of the most body-friendly forms of exercise. It is impact free and therefore kind to joints and bones, and is an extremely good source of whole body exercise, facilitating muscular contractions that are neglected during other forms of exercise. Even greater benefits can be experienced in cardiovascular efficiency, joint flexibility and muscular condition. The breathing muscles in particular – the diaphragm, and the outer and intercostal muscles – are targeted, and there is really no other form of exercise that so effectively hits these muscle groups. Consequently swimming is an ideal form of exercise for people with breathing conditions such as recurrent bronchitis or asthma. All in all, the improvements to health and the individual's quality of life can be felt almost instantaneously.

These bodily changes occur when just swimming in a pool, but when open water swimming we enter into a whole new dimension of the sport and will encounter even greater advantages. We will experience other factors such as currents, waves and the wind, three elements that add to the challenge – the effort feels harder, with the wind and the currents pushing us back and the waves crashing down on us – or we may suddenly come across a buoy we need to navigate around, or a swimmer to avoid or overtake.

At first, all this may seem to be a down side to open water swimming, with hazards and features that we wish weren't there or that we would prefer to avoid. We may wish we could just flick a switch and turn off the weather or slow down the current, move a buoy a little to the left, and get rid of all those other annoying swimmers – but with experience you will find that these are really the benefits, as they increase the excitement and enhance your workout.

From a health point of view the benefits are substantial, even over indoor swimming. In these tougher weather conditions our stabilizing muscles – the rotator cuff, serratus anterior, levator scapulae and lower trapezius – become more central in the equation: we must change our stroke pattern to go round buoys, and increase the pace to stay with the pack or overtake. All of this varies the challenge to our energy system: it avoids the repetitive strain that can be experienced in pool swimming, but in turn produces the balanced spread of work that we need.

From the perspective of rehabilitation, open water swimming is fantastic. The overuse injuries that swimmers tend to incur are less likely in open water swimmers: the fact that the stroke has to be constantly altered means that the motion is never quite the same so the muscles used are varied, and as a consequence, nothing is overused. Many of the areas that pool swimmers need to work on to ensure their musculature remains balanced (thus minimizing the risk of injury) are being taken care of whilst training specific areas – and at the same time, we are tapping into aspects of physiology that are difficult to access with other activities.

Now is the time to get started, so dive in!

CHAPTER 2

EQUIPMENT AND GETTING STARTED

One of the great things about swimming as a hobby or sport – and open water swimming is no exception to this – is that you don't need to invest large sums of money in sophisticated kit before you can take up the sport. Furthermore everything you need to enjoy your sport can be packed into and carried in a small holdall, so you can be much more flexible and spontaneous than some other popular sports such as golf, skiing or sailing, for example. Essentially all you need to start open water swimming is yourself, a stretch of water, and the will to get in and give it a go. However, in practice there are a few things that can be of help and will make the experience more pleasant.

Basic Equipment

Swimming Costume

First on your list should be a swimming costume. Although there are a few stretches of water where 'skinny dipping' is permissible, they are few and far between in the UK. This needn't be anything fancy, just something to keep your modesty. It is possible to purchase extremely expensive costumes, which claim to do all sorts of things with the aim of making you faster in the water. They do succeed in this, as can be seen in the swimsuit regulation debacle of 2008–10, when suits such as the speedo LZR racer and Blue Seventy

Nero Comp were released on to the market at the beginning of 2008. These suits work in different ways to increase a swimmer's buoyancy, the LZR suit compressing the muscles and trapping air, whereas the Nero Comp is made of special material similar to that of a wetsuit: the higher you are in the water the less resistance you create, which means you will swim faster. In 2010, FINA – the international governing body of swimming, diving, water polo, synchronized swimming and open water swimming – banned certain swimsuits from FINA-approved events, stating:

> FINA wishes to recall the main and core principle that swimming is a sport essentially based on the physical performance of the athlete.

Just as car racing is often considered nowadays to be more about the car and less about who is driving it, these suits were deemed to give such an advantage that swimming was becoming more about technology than athleticism. Records were being broken everywhere, and by a degree that had never been seen before in the history of swimming. The new FINA rules state that:

- Male swimsuits should only cover the area from the waist to the knee and women's counterparts the shoulder to the knee

- Suits must be of a 'textile' or woven material (although what they mean by 'textile' was not qualified)
- They must not have any fastening devices such as zippers (although drawstrings are allowed)

These regulations are only for FINA-approved events and thus will only affect open water swimmers competing under the auspices of that organization. In some triathlon or non FINA-approved open water swimming events, a swimskin may be allowed when a wetsuit is not: these are similar to wetsuits but not as thick, and thus not as buoyant. However, they will give you an advantage over those wearing just a regular swimsuit.

If you enjoy acquiring the latest, fanciest bit of kit for your hobby and can afford it, then you can consider buying the latest race-legal suit you can find. However, this expenditure is really not necessary in order for you to take up open water swimming – just as you don't have to buy a Ferrari in order to start driving. Unless you are competing at the highest level, such a purchase would be simply an indulgence.

Goggles

A good pair of goggles is essential. Everyone has a differently shaped face, and thus a pair that fits one swimmer will not necessarily fit another. A good test is to push the goggles gently into your eye sockets and see if they stick: if they remain in place for a few seconds, then it is likely that you have found a good match for your face shape.

When goggles are brand new they have a layer of anti-fog solution on the inner side of the lens, but over time and with use this wears off, and your goggles may start to fog up as you are swimming. This will be more noticeable when swimming in cold water. When this starts to happen it doesn't mean that you must immediately purchase a new pair, as it is possible to defog your goggles to prolong their life. There are specific anti-fog solutions applied direct to the lenses that are commercially available, or there are a couple of cheaper options that work well. The first, and a good alternative to the more expensive, commercially available products, is to coat the inner side of the lenses in toothpaste or washing-up liquid, and then wash them out – but be sure to rinse the lenses thoroughly before wearing them, as you don't want an eyeful of either substance!

The other alternative is cheaper still – in fact it is completely free! Simply spit into the lenses of your goggles, rub the spittle around,

---

PUTTING ON HAT AND GOGGLES

It is wise to wear your goggles *under* your swimming hat, as this protects them from being knocked off by another swimmer in crowded conditions. So, first place your goggle lenses on to your eye sockets, and then pull the strap over your head. Most goggles have a double strap at the back, which can be spread out on your head to ensure a sturdy hold. If you have long hair, tie this up into a ponytail first, and secure one strap above the ponytail and one below. Then put your hat on over the goggles. The seam down the middle of the hat should go down the middle of your head from front to back.

If you find that your goggles are continually slipping, wear two hats, one under your goggles and one over them.

and then rinse them out just before you enter the water.

Hats

It is advisable to wear a swimming hat in open water unless the water temperature is very hot, in which case swimming without a hat can help to cool your core temperature.

A silicon hat is a more comfortable option than a latex cap, which may pull at your hair. Cotton hats can also be used and are good in hot conditions as they will allow heat to escape from your head more efficiently, and thus lower your core temperature. For speed, however, silicon tends to be the first choice – and furthermore silicon hats will last longer than latex hats if taken care of properly: they should be washed out with fresh water each time after wearing, and left to dry at room temperature in a shady spot.

Wetsuits

Most open water swimmers will need a wetsuit. There are plenty available at greatly varying prices, and if you do want to indulge your craving to spend, here is where to put your cash.

Wetsuit fit is extremely important, and you should always try before you buy. Most wetsuit manufacturers nowadays will allow you to try a 'demo' wetsuit actually in the water before you buy, so do this if at all possible. If you cannot find anywhere that allows this, at least try on the wetsuit on dry land, and do a few arm swings or strokes to see how it fits.

Use the manufacturer's size guide to pick out a suit that you think will be a good fit. Then with the zip at the back, pull the legs of the wetsuit up your legs as you would pull on a pair of tights or leggings: the crotch must be pulled up snuggly into your crotch and all the wrinkles smoothed out. Now do the same with the arms, ensuring that they are pulled up securely all the way into your armpits. It is important to pull the crotch and armpits of the wetsuit all the way up, because if you don't, when you attempt to swim your muscles will have to work harder to overcome the resistance of the wetsuit.

Finally do up the zip; if possible, ask a friend to do this for you, as they can smooth out the zip lining and make sure that it remains smooth as they do it up. As shown in the photos, with 'normal' zips, pull the zip-pull over the top of the neck flap, and then pull the neck flap firmly, but not too tightly, across, ensuring that the male and female parts of the velcro are pushed together. With reverse zips the zip-pull can hang down loosely, though in some suits there is a small spot of velcro to which to attach it.

Apply Vaseline or some such lubricant on the back of your neck to help prevent chaffing, and you are ready to go.

The Right Size

So how do you know if you have the right size? It is normal that the wetsuit will feel restrictive and tight on land and to an extent in water, so do not decide on a suit simply because it feels comfortable on first wearing. Things to look out for that indicate a suit is too large for you include water entering at the neck or arms, or water pooling in your lower back. This is why it is preferable to try out the suit in water before you decide whether to buy.

On the other hand, if you feel your breathing is restricted because the wetsuit is tight across your chest, this would indicate that it is too small.

Remember, a wetsuit will stretch a little with wear, but it will never shrink or pull back into shape, so err on the side of too tight rather than too slack. However, if you are not satisfied with the fit, don't be afraid to try another manufacturer because, just like everyday clothes, all makes fit slightly differently.

Fig. 2.1a–g
Ensure the wetsuit is pulled fully up to your crotch.

Make surehat you pull the arms right up to your armpits.

With the zip-close flat, pull the zip up and close the velcro over the zip-pull.

Where Can I Swim?

Water, water everywhere but not a drop to swim in: it can seem like this in the UK because there are stretches of water everywhere, but it can be extremely difficult to find one that is suitable. Over the past few years many water skiing or sailing lakes have been rented out by open water swimming companies and opened to the public. If you are new to the sport this is definitely your best bet. Lifeguard cover will be provided, ensuring that the environment is as safe as can be. You don't need to worry that the stretch of water is safe to swim in because the necessary research will have been done for you – provided it is being run by a reputable company. In addition to these services you will often be provided with showers, changing rooms and toilets, and refreshments – although probably at an extra cost.

Some such venues have measured laps which you can use to test yourself, and some have organized races or training courses. However, all of this will come at a cost: first there is the financial cost – a fully serviced open water swim facility will cost much the same as, and indeed can often be slightly more than, the cost of swimming in a public pool.

Second, overcrowding can be a problem – this may seem surprising when you are looking at such a large expanse of water, especially when you are used to the local 25m pool, but at the busiest times of year the lakes may become so full of swimmers that it is not possible to achieve a decent session.

Third, opening times may be unsociable – usually swimming is only allowed very early in the morning so as to keep to a minimum any interference with the primary business of the lake. Trying to swim when the water skiers start their runs is not advisable!

If an open water swim facility is not a viable option for you – perhaps there are no such lakes in your immediate area, the opening times are unsuitable, or the costs are too high – there are, of course, stretches of water that you can swim in for free. How to go about choosing a safe, clean stretch of water where you can swim legally is fully discussed in Chapter 4, 'Situations to Avoid'.

Training Equipment

In Fig. 2.2 an assortment of training equipment is shown, which may be useful for open water swimming. In the following section each object is described, and an explanation given as to how and why it is used.

Fig. 2.2 Clockwise from the centre top: pull buoy, hand paddles, band, flippers, swim snorkel, kickboard, drag shorts.

Hand paddles: Useful to build power and strength in the arms, to aid in stroke correction, and help build feel of the water. How to use them is simple: put them on your hands (make sure you choose a left and a right) and swim. Start with sets of short repetitions and build up to longer ones.

Fins: Used to build power in the legs or to

help a slower swimmer keep up with a group that is slightly faster than them. Once again, it is obvious how to use fins – just put them on and swim. You can use them for full stroke or for leg kick only.

Neoprene shorts: An aid to the slower swimmer. A common weakness in novice swimmers is sinking legs or dropped hips. Wearing these shorts over or under the wetsuit will lift the swimmer higher in the water and thus increase their speed. They will allow swimmers who have this problem to feel what it is like to swim in the correct position in the water so they can then learn to replicate this without the shorts.

Band: Goes round the ankles. It will slow down a fast swimmer so they can train with a slower group but still get a good workout. It also allows the arms to be isolated and so build power and strength in them. The combined influence of wearing a band and using hand paddles will provide an even tougher session for the arms.

Towelly band: Essentially this is just a towel threaded through the band – see the photo. Using it will slow down a fast swimmer even more. The size of the towel should be determined by the strength of the swimmer. In combination with the hand paddles the towelly band is the ultimate workout for arm strength.

Drag shorts: Go over the wetsuit. They should be baggy enough to create extra resistance, which will make swimming more difficult. They are yet another tool to increase the difficulty of a workout or to allow a fast swimmer to train effectively with a slower group. They can be purchased specifically as 'drag shorts' from a swimming shop – though they needn't be, as any baggy pair of shorts will do, and the baggier they are, the more challenging it will be to swim with them on.

Pull buoy: A float that goes between the legs of a swimmer. In effect it is similar to the neoprene shorts in that it will lift a swimmer up in the water; it is therefore not necessary when training in a wetsuit, as the wetsuit itself will give the swimmer extra buoyancy. When using a pull buoy you should not kick your legs, as its purpose is to isolate the arms to allow you to work on this part of your stroke, and at the same time, to build strength and power. It puts less pressure on the arms alone than the paddles, band, towelly band or any combination of the three.

Kickboard: Held in front of you when you are just kicking. It isolates the leg kick and allows swimmers to concentrate on this part of their stroke in isolation. It is more difficult to use when swimming in a wetsuit due to your height in the water.

Now that you know how to choose an appropriate location to swim in, and how to use and put on the necessary equipment, you are ready to go open water swimming!

CHAPTER 3

OPEN WATER ACCLIMATIZATION

Acclimatizing to open water conditions is key in order to be successful at open water swimming, and to enjoy it. Acclimatization is especially important for beginners, whose primary aim is to become familiar and comfortable with the open water environment. Open water swimming is very different to pool swimming, and it is important to acknowledge the dissimilarities because without due circumspection it is easy to become apprehensive and overwhelmed. Here we will consider some of the differences, and discuss what we can do to condition ourselves to them, or at least to accept them.

Temperature Differences

Both extremes of temperature, whether hot or cold, are equally challenging and important. Understanding the water temperature to which you are about to expose yourself, and what steps you might take to adapt yourself to it, is essential for your enjoyment – and in extreme situations could be the difference between life and death.

We may live in a temperate climate in the UK, but unfortunately the water temperature does not usually feel that way. In general, for most of the year, most stretches of open water are unsuitable for most people to swim in without a wetsuit. But what feels comfortable can vary greatly from one swimmer to another: for example, swimming in Dover harbour in just a swimsuit may be perfectly natural for one swimmer, but to another even in a wetsuit it may feel chilly or even painful. This is due to a variety of factors including genetics, body fat percentage, and previous exposure. Nevertheless there are several ways in which you can alter your response to different water temperatures in preparation for an event.

First, wearing a swimming specific wetsuit gives an extra layer of insulation and will instantly increase comfort in cooler-than-usual temperatures such as we normally experience in the UK and Northern Europe. However, swimming in a wetsuit can take some getting used to, and choosing the correct size is vitally important if you are to feel comfortable (see Chapter 2 for more guidance on this). In some events wetsuits are not allowed regardless of the temperature – for example Channel swimming – and when training for an event such as this, cold water acclimatization will be invaluable.

Acclimatizing to Cold Water
Cold water acclimatization is when one gradually increases the duration of exposure when swimming in cold water, starting with a few minutes and eventually reaching a couple of hours – the specific duration and temperature should be determined by the race the training is for. When carrying out this procedure it is

preferable to swim in the cold twice a day. The process should run over three to four weeks, and taking cold showers during this period can increase the success and speed of your acclimatization. This may sound somewhat masochistic, but it is important to keep in mind at all times that you are doing this for a purpose, and not for enjoyment for its own sake!

If the event is to take place in particularly cold water and wearing a wetsuit is not allowed, covering your body in a thick layer of lanolin – in particular the armpits and shoulders – can immediately improve your tolerance to cold temperatures. Put the lanolin on with gloves, as it is hard to get off and will ruin your 'feel' of the water if your hands are caked in it.

There are other ways to improve your comfort instantly in cold water temperatures:

- Wear two or three thick silicon hats or a neoprene hat if allowed
- Wear a rash vest under your wetsuit
- Cover yourself in a warming cream or gel such as deep heat or tiger balm before entering the water
- Use heat pads on your lower back to keep the muscles warm and loose because if they cramp up in the cold this will inhibit your technique
- Drink a warm drink directly before and after the swim
- Wear silicon ear plugs to reduce the feeling of 'brain freeze'

In cold water situations your warm-up process is especially important. In particular you must determine if getting into the water for a 'warm-up' is a good idea – or if this will actually be more of a 'chill down'. Do not assume that a wet warm-up is preferable in all circumstances, and do not be influenced by the fact that other hardier – or perhaps more foolish

– souls venture into the water first – remember that what feels comfortable varies greatly from one person to the next.

If the water is very cold, you may decide to do a dry warm-up. For this put on your wetsuit (if it will be worn in the event) and go for a short run on land, and do plenty of arm swings and stretching to get the muscles in your arms ready for the effort ahead. Bring an elastic bungee and go through a series of rotator cuff exercises (photographs of these can be seen in Chapter 11), then a few press-ups shortly before entering the water.

If the water is so cold that you feel submerging yourself straightaway is not possible, or is likely to be such a shock as to bring you up short, run along the water's edge, first with just your feet in the water, then with the water covering your upper legs. Stop still and calmly submerge just the tip of your nose in the water for around 30 seconds, or gently splash the water up into your face four or five times: doing this will greatly reduce the shock of completely submerging your face in the cold water. Only then immerse yourself completely.

Acclimatizing to Warm Water

Warm water can be just as much of a problem as cold water, but in this situation it is hydration that is the issue, and it is important to ensure that you keep fully hydrated in the few days leading up to the event. To obtain a definitive hydration level, the urine can be tested with a refractometer, but you can get a good sense of your level of hydration by checking the colour of your own urine. If it is a dark colour it means you are dehydrated and thus need to drink more. Do not drink only pure water, however, as this is not absorbed well into the system. Consuming a water and salt solution will hydrate you more successfully, and you can buy many variations of these over the counter, or you can make your own by diluting fruit juice and adding some salt. If your urine is clear it is a good indication that you are well hydrated.

Although rare, it is possible to over-hydrate, and this can be just as dangerous as being dehydrated. Symptoms of over-hydration include muscle cramps, twitching, blurred vision and paralysis of one side of the body, none of which are good for trying to swim with. Listen to your body and you will avoid both under- and over-hydration.

In races in hot water it is more important to take advantage of feeding stations – if there are any. If there are, make sure you are familiar with their location, and what items will be available there. If there are no feeding stations but the swim is long and hot – over 45 minutes – and you are used to taking on food whilst swimming, put a gel into your costume before you start, and make a quick stop during the swim. This should take under 10 seconds, which will be quickly recovered once the nutrients are absorbed into your system and your energy levels have lifted. The salts in the gel will keep your hydration levels more stable.

As a final note, do not try any of the ideas considered here for the first time in a race, but always practise them in a safe environment first. Only then decide if you find them to be helpful or not, and thus if you will use them during a competition. Trying something for the first time in a race is both foolish and, in the context of temperature control, can be dangerous.

Swimming in a Large Pack

If you are swimming in a large pack or in close proximity to other swimmers, try not to panic: remaining calm is by far the most important thing you can do in this situation. It can feel as if people are trying to drown you as blows rain down upon you from left and right, and some may readily lose their nerve – but this may only serve to make the situation worse. If you get into real problems you can always get yourself out of danger by swimming off line into clear water, or by rolling on to your back and raising your arm. A safety boat will then come to assist you. If you are in a wetsuit you will float, so drowning should really not be a concern – although it can be hard, it is useful to remind yourself of this if you feel panic coming on.

The best way to become more at ease in this situation is to practise it regularly. If you cannot get into open water often, swim in a pool lane with two or three other swimmers on each side, to mimic pack swimming. Ask friends to swim too close to you deliberately.

Perhaps the most important manoeuvre to learn is how to swim from one side of a swimmer to the other. Once you are at ease with this you can take more control of your position in the pack and at turning points such as buoys. Practise swimming with a partner and moving from swimming on one side of them to the other. The least off-putting way for both yourself and the other swimmer is to drop back to swim at their knees, and then to swim quickly and directly over their legs and on to their other side (see Fig. 3.1—3.3).

By doing this well you will disrupt the other swimmer less. If you grab them and just swim completely over the top of them they may panic, or will be angry with you for disrupting their stroke, or both. They will be likely to strike back and then you will lose time, and you may even be disqualified. Do this regularly and you will earn yourself a bad reputation, and may find yourself being set upon in future races. But learn how to switch sides well and you will always have more control over your positioning in the group. This will give you more confidence and will lead to better turns

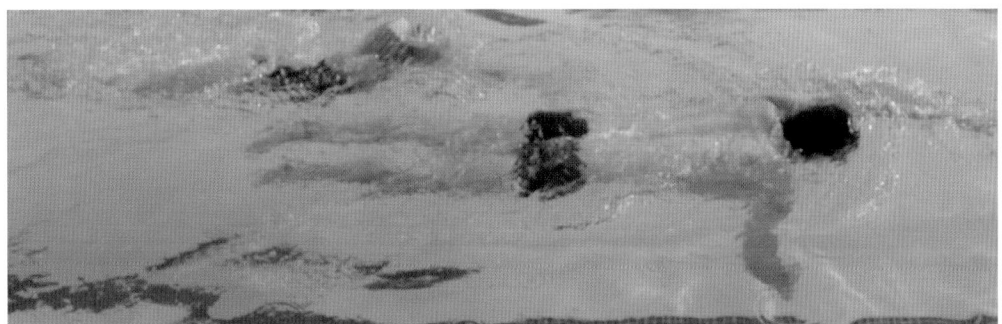

Fig. 3.1   Swim parallel with the knee of the swimmer you want to cross.

Fig. 3.2   Swim over their knees.

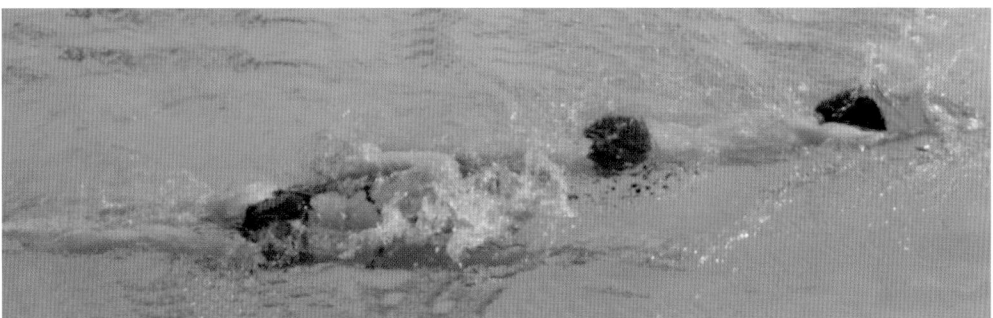

Fig. 3.3   Then regain your straight line swimming.

and exits, and thus a better overall swim and swimming experience.

Where and how you start your event can make swimming in a large pack a lot easier. Most swimmers will breathe more comfort-ably to one side than to the other. If you prefer to breathe to your right you should position yourself on the left of the start line, and conversely on the right if you prefer to breathe to the left. In times of stress – both mental and physical – we revert to actions we find to be most comfortable. The start of a race is such a time, and thus it is normal to breathe to your preferred side more than the other at this time. By positioning your start in this way you will be able to see the pack more often and more comfortably, which in turn means that you will be less likely to collide with other swimmers. We will discuss starts in greater depth in Chapter 8.

Swimming in Rough Water

Rough water makes for increased disorientation, and the feeling you get will be similar to that of swimming in a large pack. You will be knocked about, will swallow water and go off course more easily. Once again, practice makes perfect – but safety is paramount, so do not swim in rough water alone, without safety cover, or if the area has been deemed unsafe to swim in.

When swimming in rough water it is very important to learn to trust your stroke. It can feel as if you are not making headway, but if you concentrate on your technique and keep your arm turnover high, you will power through. Do not fall into the trap of matching your arm turnover to the wave speed, as this will almost certainly be too slow and you will lose time. You will need to sight more regularly, because a big wave or an area of increased tide can force you very quickly off course. If you can stay calm you will succeed. Break the swim down into bite-size pieces and focus only on getting to the next buoy or through the next 100 strokes, and then set yourself a new target to concentrate on. If you are swimming parallel to the wave direction, breathe away from the oncoming wave, otherwise you will get a mouthful of water as opposed to a lungful of air. It will be necessary to check your other side occasion-

ally, but do this with your mouth shut as a sighting movement (as discussed in Chapter 5) and not as a breath.

Swimming in Salt Water

More often than not, rough water is also salty water. This may seem a minor point to consider whilst you are sitting calmly at your desk at home or in the garden reading this book, but it is yet another factor that will increase your awkwardness in the water if you are not prepared for it. When swimming you will always take on some water, or at the very least the taste of it. In fresh water or in a swimming pool this is often not too noticeable as there is no strong taste that goes along with it, or, in the case of a swimming pool, because you have become used to the taste of chlorine. However, when taking on salty water the taste is both strong and stringent. This can be particularly unpleasant if you are swimming in a working harbour as there will be a film of diesel over the surface of the water, and if you swallow this contaminated water it can lead to stomach problems due to the increased salt content in your gut. Therefore it is more important to try to minimize water intake in salt-water conditions.

In triathlons with a salt-water swim, make sure one of your bottles on the bike is of fresh water and rinse out your mouth as soon as you get on to the bike leg.

Leaking goggles are always a problem, but in salt water the problem is intensified as the salt stings your eyes and greatly impairs vision. Make sure you have a pair of goggles that are a good fit, and that you put them on carefully, paying attention to anything coming into contact with and thus affecting the seal, such as your own hair – even one or two strands can create a debilitating leak. Remember when it comes to hair in open water swimming, tidiness is next to godliness!

Swimming Close to Boats, Kayaks or Paddleboards

If motor boats are around the taste of the water and the smell in the air won't be very pleasant, but as you cannot control this you must just accept it and focus your attention elsewhere. The best advice is to keep clear of any motorboats if you can. Most importantly, of course, do not get too close to the propellers.

It is important to know if the boat/kayak/paddleboard is taking the shortest line around the course, or if it is merely there for safety. If it is a safety boat do not follow it: it is there to watch for swimmers in difficulty, and thus will be keeping slightly apart from the swim line and will cut corners around buoys. Sight your own route and avoid coming into too close a contact with the boat – but most importantly do not let it affect your route.

If the boat/kayak/paddleboard is leading the pack and taking the best route around the course, you can use this to sight, provided you are near enough to the front of the pack to see it clearly. It is still important not to blindly follow the guide boat and to check occasionally that your route is correct, but you are allowed the luxury of doing this much less frequently than would usually be necessary. On the majority of your sights you can sight purely the lead boat/kayak/paddleboard, and as this object will be closer to you than the buoy, this will take less effort.

In longer events, such as a Channel swim, you will need a boat with you both for your own safety and to provide you with food. You must practise swimming with this boat, and if possible with the people who will be controlling it, so that you learn how to work well together. You will also need to practise taking on food from the boat, as this skill will be vitally important.

Weeds, Fish and Jellies

When you first start swimming in open water the 'hazards' of weeds, fish and jellies will be unusual and can seem daunting. However, none present a real difficulty, and as with most aspects of open water swimming, the key is to get used to them so that they do not disturb your focus on the swim itself. In most open water situations you will be the biggest fish by far and so most definitely the top of the food chain. It is very much a case of 'they are more scared of you than you are of them'. If you are not the biggest fish, then anything bigger than you must be friendly, otherwise you should not be swimming in the particular stretch of water you are in – Great Whites are to be avoided! So as far as fish are concerned, the message is, don't worry about them.

In some areas of sea, jellyfish are present. These tend to stay in packs, which means that if you come across a few, you are likely to come across a lot. In the United Kingdom most do not sting, and in general those that do are not dangerous. If you know the jellyfish to be non-stinging, keep your focus on your swimming and don't worry about the jellies. However, some people can be allergic to stings from the stinging variety. If you know you are, then stay well clear, because anaphylactic shock whilst swimming is definitely not ideal! Outside the United Kingdom jellyfish can be lethal, so it is important that you do your research before you jump in.

Weeds, for some reason, instill a great deal of fear for the beginner open water swimmer. This may be due to various stories in fiction in which someone drowns after 'getting caught in the weeds'. However, the types of fresh-

and salt-water weeds found in and around the UK are most unlikely to be strong enough to challenge a competent swimmer, so there is really no need to be frightened. Nevertheless, even though there is no rational reason to be afraid of weeds, you should still try to avoid them as best you can, as they will interrupt your stroke and slow you down if you become tangled in them.

It can be of benefit to take some time in a warm-up or warm-down, when you are calm and not in a rush, to make a point of coming into close contact with weeds and any fish that are around, because you will then see that there is nothing to be afraid of.

Reaching Your Goal

In most situations it can be calming to consider yourself as just being in a big swimming pool. Once you have understood, encountered and mastered all the extra variables thrown at you that we have considered in this chapter, this is essentially the situation you will find yourself in. You will have overcome any fears, and will be able to swim successfully in all kinds of open water environments. You will be on your way to reaching your open water goal.

CHAPTER 4

SITUATIONS TO AVOID

There are several situations that should be avoided when swimming in open water, the most significant being rip tides, polluted water, cramps, and lost goggles or swimming hats. The media reports at length about the dangers of wild or open water swimming, and consequently it would be easy to assume that imminent death was likely the moment you place your toes into open water. The reality is thankfully rather different. Certainly there are risks, but like any other outdoor sport, open water swimming is only dangerous if undertaken irresponsibly and without due care being paid to risk assessment.

Therefore before entering a new stretch of water, run through your checklist as follows: is it safe; is it clean; and is it legal? If the answer to these three questions is 'yes', then it is time to get wet.

Safety

If other people are swimming already in a certain water, or you have previously seen others swimming there, it is likely that the spot is safe. However, conditions will change from day to day, so it is important to evaluate the safety of the area on the individual day that you plan to swim.

Firstly consider the weather: Is it particularly windy, or has there been a significant change in rainfall? An increase in rainfall will make flowing water flow faster and can result in a drop in temperature, while a decrease in rainfall will cause the water level to be lower, which could mean that you are swimming in closer proximity to pipes or rocks – it is important to pay attention to this. If there is lightning, do not get into the water.

Check your entry and exit points: If you are planning to swim downriver and then return on foot to your starting point, start your assessment at your chosen exit point, and walk back upstream to your starting point. This way you can view the entire stretch you will swim before you enter the water. Make a particular note of a feature that you will see and can use as a marker just before your exit point so that you do not swim past it – swimming back upriver against the current may be more difficult than you think.

Assess the route: When assessing the route you plan to take on a river, or in the sea for that matter, look for obstacles – rocks, fallen branches, discarded prams – and places where the water either speeds up or slows down. You can often spot these by looking at the surface of the water – an area of ruffled water can often indicate shallows or a more rapid current.

Do not jump into the water: If you can see the bottom it is likely to be too shallow, and if you can't, it means objects may be lurking below. Rather, step in carefully from the bank.

Avoid reservoirs: Although many mass swim events have been held in reservoirs, which suggests they are safe for swimming, this is often not the case. Many have high walls that can be hard or impossible to get out of; they are deeper than lakes and therefore can be colder; and in some there is machinery, which makes them unsuitable for swimming in.

Cleanliness

You can get a general answer as to how clean a water is simply by looking at and smelling it. More detailed information can be found on the Environment Agency website (see Further Information at the end of the book). You can put in the postcode of the area you wish to swim in, and will find detailed information on various topics such as bathing water quality, the risk of flooding from reservoirs, river and sea levels, and river quality.

Whilst rivers in the UK are the cleanest they have been for 150 years, there are still two main areas of concern, both of which are widely misunderstood: Weill's disease and blue-green algae.

Weill's disease: The threat of contracting Weill's disease is still present. It is most often picked up close to the banks when entering or exiting the water, and although it is not very common, its effects, if it is contracted, can be very debilitating. To reduce as much as is possible the likelihood of contracting it, cover up open wounds; seek the help of your doctor if you contract flu-like symptoms up to three weeks after swimming.

Blue-green algae: There is a considerable, and justifiable, fear of this algae in the UK, although with moderate care the risk can be limited and/or avoided. If swum through or swallowed, blue-green algae can be toxic to both animals and humans and can result in a rash, eye irritation, fever, diarrhoea, vomiting, and muscle and joint pains. There are no records of human deaths due to blue-green algae, but contact can be fatal for some animals.

The algae can develop in any fresh warm water, but the blooms are often highly visible and thus can be avoided. The water may look like jelly or paint and will be blue/green or green/brown in colour. Often a musty earthy smell will be present. If the blooms are evident there is about a 50 per cent chance that the algae will be toxic, so it is best to avoid it. This does not mean that it is necessary to keep clear of the entire stretch of water, just to avoid the bloom. Many mass events take place successfully with blue-green algae present, and the blooms are simply swept away from the course.

The Law

Currently the laws on swimming in open water in the United Kingdom are being clarified. At present it is legal to swim in open water unless you are trespassing on the adjoining land, so it is the access to the water, rather than the water itself, which is the issue. You should therefore ensure that you enter the water from a public path.

Angling clubs which own the fishing rights to a particular stretch of water own just those, and not the actual water itself, and therefore you have the right to swim. Having said that, you can expect that they will not be too happy if you disturb their fish. Also, while you have the right to swim, they also have the right to fish, and it will not do your expensive new wetsuit any good if a fishhook pulls a lump out of it! If you see people fishing it pays dividends to approach them and ask where it is safe to swim so that you will not disturb their fishing – but be prepared to be firm if they assert their exclusive right to the enjoyment of the water.

Similarly houses that border a lake or river own only the riverbed or lake edge and not the water, so once again you have the right to swim.

It is legal to swim in any navigable water – that is, water where boats can pass – but do ensure that you are clearly visible if you choose to do this, as the boat skipper may not be expecting to see a swimmer in his or her path – so wear a brightly coloured swimming hat, and raise your head at regular intervals to look around. Remember that power may give way to sail, but swimmers give way to everything!

In Scotland you have the right to swim in any open space.

Further undesirable situations and how to avoid or cope with them are explained below.

Temperature and Avoiding Cramps

In the United Kingdom the primary risk when swimming outdoors is the cold. When the body gets cold, blood is redirected to the core to maintain vital organs, and when this happens the extremities, and in particular the arms and legs, weaken, which means that you lose strength and power. It is important to allow yourself to acclimatize to the cold water, as has been explained in Chapter 3. Wearing a wetsuit provides insulation and therefore warmth as well; it also increases buoyancy, thus decreasing the effort needed to move through the water, and thereby minimizing the risk of becoming too fatigued.

In foreign countries the heat can be as much of a problem as the cold is in the United Kingdom. In hot water you will become dehydrated quickly, which can result in cramps.

Although the exact physiology behind cramping is currently unknown, it is thought that the risk of cramping is increased by dehydration and in particular a lack of potassium and magnesium. Drinking isotonic drinks or taking magnesium and potassium supplements can decrease the likelihood of developing cramps. Bananas contain high levels of potassium and are a healthy pre- or post-swim snack. Cramps can be very dangerous to the open water swimmer if panic sets in, and if you do suffer a cramp whilst swimming it is important to stay calm. Cramps often pass on their own, but you can speed up their passing by calmly stretching out the affected area. Staying aware of what is going on is vital to get you through the cramp safely.

Lost Goggles or Swimming Hats

Losing your goggles whilst swimming can be very disorientating. This has happened to all swimmers at some point, and the likelihood of losing your goggles is increased during a mass swim. Wearing your goggles underneath your swimming hat decreases the risk of them being completely knocked off. You should also regularly check the strap for deterioration so as to reduce the likelihood of it breaking. It is useful to practise swimming without your goggles on occasionally, but in a safe and controlled environment so that if they fall off or snap in the middle of a race you know you will still be able to swim safely.

If your goggles start to leak during an event it is possible to lift them off your face when coming up for a breath or to sight, and to empty the water out; then firmly push them back on to your face. If you have nimble fingers you should be able to do this fairly easily with a bit of practice whilst swimming normally on your front; if you struggle, then roll on to your back. This will give you more time, but beware, because lying on your back with your arm raised is a signal to the rescue cover that you are in trouble – so try not to remain in this position for too long.

To most men, and to girls with short hair, losing your hat does not represent a particular problem unless you are relying on it to maintain your body warmth. But to those with long hair, swimming without a hat can be difficult because hair whips round in front of your eyes, making it hard to see, and into your mouth making it hard to breathe. Tightly tying up your hair underneath your swimming hat provides a fall-back position should your hat come off in the swim, and this strategy should be sufficient to keep your eyes and airways clear. If the water is not too hot, wearing two swimming hats, one underneath and one over your goggles, means that even if you do lose one hat your hair will still be tightly contained within the second.

It is also advisable not to wear a brand new cap or a very old (stretched out) one in a race situation. Keep spares in your bag so that if your hat falls off, goes missing, or rips in training you always have a back-up.

Swimming in Tidal Water

If swimming in tidal water, research the tide times. These can be found on the BBC website along with detailed coastal forecasts. Be aware that the pull of the tide will be at its weakest close to high or low tide – approximately an hour either side – so this is the safest time to swim, as the effects of the tide on your progress will be less. Getting back to shore when the tide is going out will be harder and is unwise for beginners, so you should plan to complete your swim before high tide.

If swimming in water subject to currents, it is necessary to determine the strength and direction of the current before getting into the water. This can be difficult to do, and often little information can be gained by simply looking at the water. If there are buoys or boats moored in the water these can be useful to determine the strength of the tide or current by looking at how the water rushes around and pulls these. Other than this, dropping a stick into the water and seeing how it is affected can be useful, but information gleaned from this should be interpreted on the side of caution because the direction and strength of the tide varies with time over the tide cycle, so what you see now may not be the same as what you will experience in your swim.

You need to be able to predict what the water will be doing in an hour's time from what it is doing when you observe it from the shore. As a general rule the water is slack around high or low tides, and then picks up speed so that it is at its maximum half way between these. The time gap between high and low tides is usually six hours, but this can vary. As the water picks up speed its course around obstacles such as rocks or little bays or headlands can change.

One of the most important facts to ascertain, and this will not be found on the BBC website, is the strength of the tide when it is running at its fullest, because this can dictate whether it is safe to swim there or not. I can well remember training with a very strong swimmer in the Blackwater estuary in Essex where the tides are strong, and recall his surprise when he found, twenty minutes into the swim, that he was still in exactly the same place as when he set off. A lesser swimmer would have found himself a mile downstream by then!

There is really no substitute for local knowledge, so if you can, ask the advice of a local fisherman or sailor. If you can gain access to a local sailing club you may find tide charts

RIP TIDES

If you are caught in a rip tide (and for this purpose I include any tide which you are finding it difficult to swim against) and find yourself getting into difficulties, turn and head straight for the shore. If the current is running along the shore, as it will be in a river estuary, this will result in you reaching the shore several hundred metres from where you wanted to be – but at least you will be safe, and this is the shortest route to safety.

pinned up on the walls there. Other than this, teenage boys can prove to be a vault of local knowledge as far as waterways go.

When first getting into water subject to currents or tides a little information will get you a long way, and it is advisable to observe the following guidelines if you hope to tackle water affected by tides or currents successfully:

- Keep close to the bank if swimming upstream against the current, because the pull from the current or tide is weakest in shallower water
- Swim in the middle of the river or further out to sea when swimming downstream, with the current, because the pull from the current or tide is strongest in deeper water

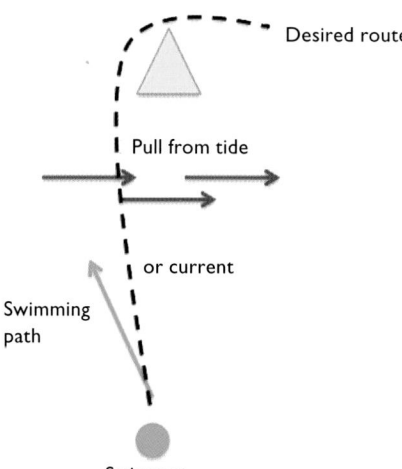

Fig. 4.1 Swimming on course with the tide pulling you inside the turn buoy

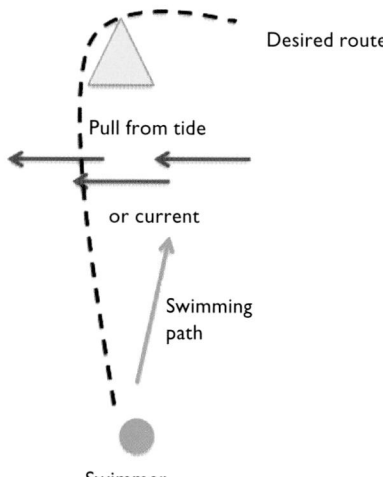

Fig. 4.2 Swimming on course with the tide pulling you outside the turn buoy.

SITUATIONS TO AVOID

- If swimming across the current or tide to a buoy or exit point, ensure that you adjust your trajectory accordingly (see diagram below)
- Be aware that it is harder to swim into shore when the tide is going out

As can be seen from this, planning your course in a swimming race in the open sea can make a huge difference to the effective distance you travel, and the key to this is understanding precisely what the tide will be doing on each part of the course at the stage you swim over it. Even the local sailors and fishermen will probably know little about the vagaries of the currents close inshore, which is where you will be near the start or finish of the race. If you are serious about such a race you really need to visit the area, preferably in a boat, on at least one previous tide cycle so that you can measure the strength and direction of the tide at the various stages of the cycle. But be careful to translate what you discover to the correct part of your race. Tide times progress at roughly one hour a day, so if, for instance, you find that the tide flows from right to left at 2 knots at 2pm today, it will probably be doing the same tomorrow at around 3pm.

CHAPTER 5

SIGHTING

Sighting is the skill used to ensure that you are swimming in a straight line when open water swimming. It is one of the most important aspects of open water swimming, and one of the trickiest to master.

Firstly let us consider why sighting is so important. An open water swimming course is a route from one point to another, whether this is round inflatable buoys or between landmarks, and everyone completing the event has to swim round the same course in the same direction. Irrespective of how many buoys or landmarks you are to navigate, the shortest distance around the course is in a straight line from one buoy or landmark to the next. Poor sighting will decrease your chances of taking the shortest route, whilst an athlete with good sighting skills will complete the swim from start to finish by covering a shorter total distance.

It is fairly easy to see where you are going whilst swimming, but to see where you are going without unduly disrupting the efficiency of your swim is challenging. There are two distinct methods commonly used for sighting, imaginatively called the 'beginner' method and the 'advanced' method.

Sighting for Beginners

For beginner open water swimmers there is a significant balance between seeing where you are going and maintaining swimming efficiency. It is common to see beginners stop-ping and treading water to sight, but clearly this stop-start approach results in rather inefficient swimming. A balance between efficiency and seeing where you are going can be achieved by the following method:

- Swim front crawl for around twenty strokes. During these strokes breathe as you normally would
- After the twenty front crawl strokes, transition immediately to three or four strokes of breaststroke with your head out of the water. If you prefer you can use doggy paddle for this, but it is obviously less efficient
- During these 'head out' strokes, scan the horizon to get your bearings, orientate your body correctly, and then recommence front crawl strokes

As long as you continue to make forward progress whilst your head is out of the water you will maintain a reasonable degree of swimming efficiency.

As a beginner open water swimmer it is advisable to practise this method in the swimming pool before trying it in open water. When doing so, focus on a smooth transition from front crawl to breaststroke (or doggy paddle), and back to front crawl again. It is also important to get used to the change in balance, orientation and visibility you will experience from swimming with your head in the water as opposed to out of the water.

If you are accompanied by a friend you

can practise focusing on small objects in the distance by asking them to stand at the end of the swimming pool and hold up an A4 piece of paper with a number between one and ten written on it. When you move into your head-out strokes, focus on the piece of paper and report the number back to your friend when you get to the end of the length.

Sighting for More Advanced Swimmers

The advanced sighting method is as simple as lifting your head as you swim. As you are swimming, lift your head so that your eyes are just above the waterline and you can see forwards – the smaller the movement, the more efficient it is. To improve your efficiency yet further, arch your back so that your hips, legs and feet stay near the surface of the water: like this you can maintain a more horizontal body position in the water, which is the fastest and most efficient way to swim. Once you lower your head back into the water, return to a neutral spine and horizontal swimming position.

Fig. 5.1a–c Lift your head so that only your eyes clear the water, keeping an arch in your lower back whilst doing so in order to increase swimming efficiency.

It is important to sight regularly, because you can very quickly end up well off course, costing you valuable time and energy: using this method it is advisable to sight about every six strokes. As a more advanced swimmer you are progressing through the water more quickly, and a small error of alignment can quickly turn into you being well off course, so more frequent sighting is advisable. Further to this, I recommend less frequent sighting for beginner swimmers as the action of sighting itself takes a great deal more effort for beginners and will slow them down more. If, during your sight, you find that you are directly on course, then sight again in around six strokes; but if you do not see your marker, or if you are off course, sight again every two strokes until you get your bearings back and are on course.

By sighting with a six-stroke frequency you can also incorporate a breath into the motion. When your hand (either left or right) enters the water above your head, press down slightly and arch your back to help you to lift your head until your eyes are just out of the water. Almost immediately turn your head to the side (the same side as the arm you used to press down on the water at the start of the motion) to breathe: you will easily have time to take a normal breath before you have completed the recovery phase of this same stroke. Incorporating your breath into the sighting motion like this means you will lose almost no momentum and will therefore maintain greater swimming efficiency.

As with the beginner method, practise initially in the swimming pool, and make use of friends to spot things in the distance, as discussed above.

Sighting in Different Types of Water

Once you have mastered either the begin-ner or the advanced method of sighting in the swimming pool, make sure to practise it in all open water conditions: salty, fresh, rough, calm, hot and cold, and both with and without a wetsuit. Remember that so much concerning open water swimming is about familiarization and preparation.

SIGHTING WITH A WETSUIT

When sighting with a wetsuit you may find that the zip fold rubs on the back of your neck. Applying some anti-chaffing lubrication before entering the water should stop this becoming a problem.

Sighting in particularly choppy water can be tricky, and it is important to time your sighting with the rolling of the waves. If you attempt to sight just before you hit a wave, all you will see is a big wall of water. By timing your sight correctly you should get a good view from the top of the wave. However, this takes practice, and initially it may be necessary to lift your head a little higher, and so arch your back a little more, and sight more frequently.

Using Points on the Land to Sight

The easiest objects to see when swimming are those that are high up and those that are large. Using landmarks, or objects on the land, to sight can be extremely helpful in very rough swims, or swims where the markers are small or of a poor colour so they blend in with the water, sky or backdrop. When sighting efficiently you have only a millisecond when your eyes are out of the water to orientate yourself with the course. Something big and distinctive on the horizon can be easier to see in that time frame than the markers that are often used to indicate the route of an open water swimming course.

It is important that the object you choose is not something that is going to move. Suitable objects are tall buildings, barns, houses with distinctively coloured gable ends, trees, lamp-posts, electricity pylons, telegraph poles – the list is endless. But as long as the object is immovable, in line with your route, and stands out on the horizon, it is suitable.

Before you start your swim have a look on the horizon and try to decide which objects may be suitable. If you are competing in an event where you are able to practise on the course first, or can get into the water for a warm-up, use this time to orientate yourself with the course and to find suitable markers on the land which you can use to sight your way round the course. If you get a chance to do this on the day before the race, so much the better; you can then build these landmarks into your visualization of the race so that you know exactly what to expect when you hit the water. (For more on visualization, see Chapter 6.)

CHAPTER 6

COMPETITIVE OPEN WATER SWIMMING

Open water swimming is a welcoming and healthy outdoor activity to take part in. It need not be competitive or stressful, and no matter how old or young, how fit or unfit you are, you are always welcome to just have a swim around for exercise, to practise your stroke or to explore the water. However, if you are of a more competitive mind-set there are many organized open water swimming events which allow you to race your peers, and yourself, and will help you to progress to a higher level of swimming and racing.

One of the great things about open water swimming events is that there are generally large numbers of competitors of all abilities taking part. There are no heats and so you do not always need to race to win, but instead can focus and enjoy achieving your short-term goals in the company of other enthusiasts. Regardless of your current level and your goals, there is sure to be an event out there for you.

How to Find an Event

Nowadays there is a plethora of open water swimming events available to you. Simply ask another open water swimmer, and it is likely that they will know of some established events that are scheduled in the near future. Further to this, most races are advertised on the internet and thus can be found easily by entering a search for open water swimming races in your local area. If you train regularly at an organized open water swimming venue, then there may even be 'in house' races held there.

Open water swimming has become extremely popular in the past few years, and there are many professional organizations involved in putting on races open to all levels. These of course have the advantage of having the support and back-up of the organizer behind them, so you can be confident that the water and access to it are safe, there will be plenty of facilities (such as toilets), and that the safety boats and first aid centres will be adequately manned. There may also be stalls run by local or national sports retailers, which provide a great opportunity to research any item of kit you may be interested in investing in. Indeed, the company which organizes the Great North Run currently also runs an event called the 'Great Swim', which consists of a series of open water swimming events held at different locations around the United Kingdom. These can be great if you fancy using your hobby as an excuse to see some of the country. Further to this there is always an elite wave scheduled for the day during which you can watch professional open water swimmers compete on the same course as you! Although this particular series of events is relatively beginner-friendly, they do attract large numbers of entrants, with the result that it can feel a little like you are swimming in a washing machine. Consequently, unless you are feeling particularly confident, the best advice is to take part in a smaller local race before tackling this national event.

Pre-race Packing: Your Kit Bag

The week before your race you should start thinking about what you need to take with you. It is important not to overpack. Taking too many things with you will not only be

Table 1   Items you will need

Always	Cold Weather	Hot Weather
Race entry confirmation	Warm clothing for before and after	Sun protection cream
Photographic identification	Extra thick swimming hat or or neoprene hat	Umbrella for shade
Swimsuit or trunks	Thermos of warm drink	Extra electrolyte drinks
Swimming hat	Heat patch for back (must try this out in training)	Extra water
Spare swimming hat	Rash vest for under wetsuit (if allowed ***)	
Goggles	Heating cream	
Spare pair of goggles	Spare socks to keep on your hands and feet until the last minute before the start	
Wetsuit (if the event allows*)	Stretch cords to use as a warm-up if it is too cold to get into the water to warm up	
Anti-chaffing cream		
Rubber gloves or small plastic bag (to apply anti-chaffing cream with **)		
Towel x 2		
Electrolyte drink		
Water		

* If the water is above a certain temperature you may not be allowed to compete in a wetsuit. It is unusual that the water in the United Kingdom reaches this level, so a wetsuit is likely to be a regular component of your kit. However, if you are unsure, check with the event staff well in advance of the race so you can properly train and prepare for the event.

**Avoid getting this cream on to your hands. It is non-water-soluble and thus hard to wash off. If it is on your hands and you touch your goggles you are likely to then transfer the cream on to the goggles, which will then be near impossible to see through.

***In some triathlons you are only allowed to wear these underneath your trisuit and so must complete the whole event in the rash vest if you start in it. If this is the case, think carefully about whether you will warm up during the other disciplines. Over-heating in a race will substantially slow you down.

heavy and impractical, it will make it more difficult to find the items you actually need on the morning of the race. So be selective. In Table 1 I have drawn up a list of items that you will need to take with you; for ease of reference I have split this into three categories: 'Always', 'Cold Weather' and 'Hot Weather'.

Arriving at the Race

It is important to arrive at the race venue in good time for your event. However, arrive too early and you are likely to be tired by the time your event starts. Spending time at a race venue can be stressful: the tension in the air from other competitors can be a brilliant way to stir you up and get you going, but you don't want to be exposed to this for too long as it will significantly fatigue you.

Depending on the size of the event (in terms of the number of entrants queuing at race reception) and the size of the venue – estimated by factors such as the distance between the car park and the registration desk, the changing facilities and the swim start – it should be enough to arrive between ninety minutes to two hours before your race start.

Warming Up

At some open water swimming events you will be able to get into the water to warm up, at others you will not. Research this first so that you can practise your warm-up in training.

Wet Warm-up
If you are able to get into the water to warm up and it is not too cold then you are lucky and can carry out a wet warm-up. My sugges-

tion would be to get into the water fifteen to twenty minutes prior to your start time, and spend about seven minutes swimming aerobically and just getting used to the water and the surroundings. During this time gradually increase your pace so that you are fully warm by the end of your seven minutes.

Pay attention to what you can see in the water and what you can't, and ideally line up some sighting landmarks to guide you around the course (see Chapter 5). If the event is being held in tidal water or water subject to currents, use this time to determine the strength of the currents and the direction they are going in. You will need to use this information in the race and keep to shallow water when swimming against the current or tide, and in deeper water when swimming with the current or tide (see Chapter 4). Also practise adjusting your trajectory when heading for the course markers to take account of the pull from the current or tide.

Once you are sufficiently warm, carry out around five bursts of twenty strokes fast, and swim back into shore. Don't spend too long on shore before your event as you will begin to cool down and stiffen up in this period. Try to keep moving, swinging your arms and carrying out a few practice arm strokes in the air.

When you are called, head to the start and line up in the knowledge that your body is fully warmed up and ready to go.

Dry Warm-up
In many open water swimming and triathlon events you are not able to get into the water before the event and so need to carry out a dry warm-up, on land. You may also wish to carry out this kind of warm-up if the water that the event is being held in is extremely cold, for instance 14°C or below. In this case you should try to bring some stretch cords with you. The aim will be to warm up your

body, speeding up nerve synapses, and then to encourage blood into your arms prior to the event.

Going for a short jog whilst in your wetsuit or swimming gear underneath warmer layers is a great way to generally warm up your body. After a short jog (again, around seven minutes should be enough time), start thinking more specifically about warming up your upper body.

If you have them, set up your swimming cords and spend a few minutes carrying out some arm strokes with these; then swing your arms and repeat this. If you don't have swimming cords you can simulate this by setting up a theraband in a similar way – therabands can be bought from any good physiotherapist practice or swimming equipment shop. Finish off by a few more powerful strokes with the bands and some quick practice arm strokes in the air.

As with your wet warm-up, do not stand around for a long time after your warm-up waiting for your race, but try to time it so that you have finished warming up just a few minutes before your race starts. If you finish early keep moving, swinging your arms and carrying out a few practice strokes in the air.

The Psychology of the Race

When you enter your event, write down your goal of what you want to achieve during it. These should be SMART targets, as explained in Chapter 10: a finishing position, a time you want to beat, or simply to hold good technique or to stay calm in the lead-up to the race – all of these are good targets. Use these goals to focus your training. During the week before your event remind yourself of these targets, and spend some time visualizing yourself achieving them. Feel how you will feel when you do.

Visualization is an incredibly useful tool in race preparation, and can significantly influence your performance and thus the outcome of the race. It is also useful to visualize a few different scenarios where things don't run exactly to plan: think how you will cope with these, and still finish up achieving your goal. Once you have worked out your strategy for the specific scenario being considered, rewind your imaginary visualization tape and rerun it, this time with you coping with the problem. Never visualize a negative outcome – or at least never leave a visualization without rerunning it to a successful conclusion.

At the event it can be easy to get carried away with nerves. A certain amount of nervousness is good as it gets your adrenalin pumping, but too much can be destructive: let your nerves get the better of you, and you are beaten before you start. Try to keep focused, and don't allow yourself to pay too much attention to what others are doing. Everyone has their own method of controlling their nerves, and you need to find one that works for you, but it generally pays at some point in the run-up to the start to find a quiet space to get changed and prepare yourself mentally.

Spend a few minutes visualizing yourself achieving your goal. Follow your nutrition programme, and if you find it helps calm you down, listen to some music. The choice of music is very much a personal one: some find that listening to more upbeat music is a good way to get them into a fighting frame of mind; others prefer calm mood music. Use the warm-up to relax your mind, but also to focus on the task ahead.

Whatever method you adopt, you must learn to turn it off when you are called down to the start line. This is the time to let all other thoughts and worries leave your mind so you just focus on what you are about to do and on achieving your goal.

The Race Itself

With so many swimmers in the water, when the starter shouts 'On your marks – Go!', blows a start whistle or fires a starting gun, there is pandemonium: that tense calm just before the start explodes into a churning mass of white water. Beginners must first learn not to be overwhelmed by this, but instead to harness the energy of the mass start.

For the more experienced competitor, the sound of a starting gun seems to flick a switch inside them. We forget all our well rehearsed plans of pacing ourselves, and go flat out. Try to taper this in. Yes, it is necessary to go off fast and not get blocked behind other slower swimmers, but don't go off at your 50m sprinting, all-out pace. Always keep in mind that you have to complete the whole swim, or the whole triathlon if that is the event you are competing in.

At around 400m it is quite common to feel as if an elephant has just jumped on your back and is dragging you down. However, at this point try to relax as much as possible and focus on your technique. This feeling will pass, so take comfort from the knowledge that everyone is feeling this way.

When things feel tough, remember your goal and all the work you have put in to get you to this point. Remember all the people who have helped you to get here, and keep on pushing forwards. It will pay off when you finish and can relax and enjoy the satisfaction of having accomplished your SMART target.

After the Race

If possible carry out a short warm-down in the water to flush out all the toxins that your body has released as you fought your way around the course. If you cannot get back into the water a short jog is a good substitute.

Follow the post-race nutrition guidelines as described in Chapter 9.

Finally, relax and feel proud!

CHAPTER 7

SWIM DRAFTING

Swim drafting is a technique that can be used in open water swimming either to make you swim faster than you normally could, or to allow you to use less energy when swimming at the same speed. Studies have shown that by swimming directly behind (drafting on the feet) or to the side (drafting on the hip) of another swimmer it is possible to use between 18 and 25 per cent less energy.

The principle is the same as bike drafting. By sitting behind or to the side of another swimmer you are swimming within their bow wave; there is less resistance from the water here, and by being in this position you get sucked forwards in the water that they are pulling along with them. As long as you are within another swimmer's bow wave you will have to exert less energy to move forwards. The most efficient position to be in is as close as possible to the side of, and slightly in front of, the hip of the fastest swimmer in the pack.

As always, practice makes perfect, and practice is definitely necessary when attempting to draft effectively. Practising over the winter in the swimming pool is advisable as it will allow you to practise your skills in a controlled environment. However, make sure you ask a partner before you start your drafting practice, as drafting directly behind or next to just any swimmer in a public lane will certainly not end well!

The Reasons for Drafting

Quite simply, drafting saves you energy. You are pulled forwards by the water that the adjacent swimmer is already moving through, burning his own energy. Due to this you need to use less energy to make forward progress yourself, and thus you will either arrive at the finish point of your swim more quickly, or

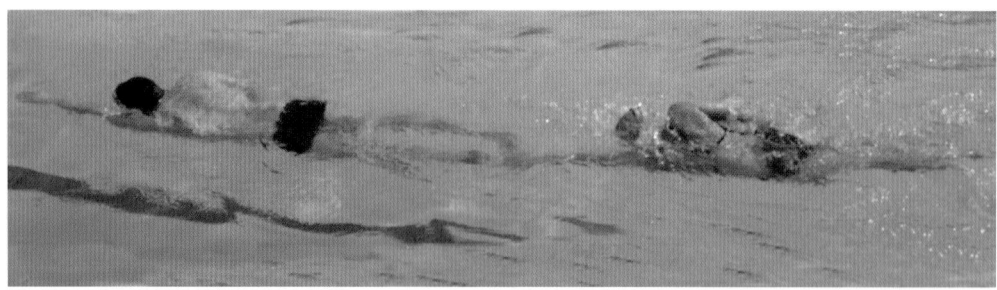

Fig. 7.1   Swim as close to the feet of the swimmer in front as is possible without disturbing either of your strokes.

Fig. 7.2   Swim as close as possible to the side of the swimmer next to you, staying in the nook between their hip and shoulder.

having used less energy than you could without the 'draft'.

As mentioned in the first paragraph, there are two main places where you can position yourself in order to draft effectively: on the feet of the swimmer in front, or on their hips.

Drafting on the Feet

In this method you swim directly behind someone, with your body as close as possible to their feet (see Fig. 7.1). The closer you are to their feet, the more benefit you will get, though be careful because if you are too close you may get a swift kick to the face, or you may slow down their (and therefore your own) progress by disturbing their leg kick.

Drawbacks
When swimming directly on another swimmer's feet it can be tempting not to sight and to blindly follow their route. However, it is important to keep checking that you are on line. When drafting behind an unknown or new swimmer you should keep up your regular sighting for a short period (around 100m

should be enough to determine whether the swimmer's route is to be trusted or not). If the swimmer is taking a good path and not wavering about too much you may then reduce your sighting frequency. Nevertheless it is still important to continue to sight about every six or twenty strokes, as fully explained in Chapter 5. The responsibility of the route taken and of your swim is still your own, so do not fall into the trap of being lazy and completely trusting the route set by others.

It can be more difficult to sight past the swimmer in front because you will need to lift your head further out of the water to ensure that you can see over them. Practise doing this in the pool to get a feeling for how high is high enough. Lifting your head higher than this will only waste valuable energy. Using static landmarks to sight will also mean you do not need to lift your head so high, and therefore swimming in this fashion will save you energy.

Another drawback is that your catch will be less effective, because the water that you will be pulling and pushing to move yourself forwards is less dense due to the movement of the feet of the swimmer in front creating air bubbles. However, if done correctly the benefits of this technique will far outweigh the drawbacks.

Drafting on the Hip

When drafting on the hip you should be swimming slightly behind the adjacent swimmer with your head in line with their chest (see Fig. 7.2). In this position you get the most benefit, as more of your body is within their bow wave. However, this technique takes a little more practice than drafting on the feet. Moreover, swimming here will slow down your draftee as they will need to exert more energy to pull you forwards with them, so you may therefore expect some reaction from them – they will either swim away from you, or swim across you to break the draft, or will retaliate more directly.

It is advisable to breathe towards the swimmer you are drafting off because then you can keep an eye on how close you are, and on what they are doing. Once again, it is important to stay as close as possible without disturbing the swimmer you are drafting off. In a sense you are getting a free ride, so swim as nicely as possible next to them. Not only is this good sportsmanship, but it will help to ensure they don't get too annoyed and swim away from you or – worse still – directly over you to get you out of their wake.

An additional benefit to this position is that you can tuck in quite neatly between the swimmer's armpit and torso and so when breathing towards them you should be able to get a nicely sheltered breath. Sighting is also easier in this position than when drafting on the feet because you don't need to sight over another swimmer and so don't need to raise your head as high out of the water.

Drawbacks

When done correctly there are no real drawbacks to this method of drafting. However, there are some mistakes that are easy to make, in which case the experience may become rather unpleasant.

If you are swimming on the hip of a good swimmer then their hand exit will be below the hip and thus perfectly lined up with your face. It is best to position yourself slightly in front of the hip to ensure you are not struck. Not only is being slapped in the face unpleasant, and the impact annoying to the draftee, but importantly, this is when your goggles are most at risk from being knocked off your face.

Also, if you are swimming in this position but out of time with the arm stroke of the other swimmer you are sure to clash hands at some point. This is a minor issue but it will slow you down, it can push you off target, and it will annoy your draftee, meaning they may try to swim away from you.

As ever, the advice is to practise swimming in time with the swimmer next to you during training to get the most out of your draft.

CHAPTER 8

STARTS, EXITS AND TURNING AROUND BUOYS

Starts

Different events have different starting procedures. Amateur triathletes are most likely to start their event from a deep water floating start behind a start line, or in the water holding on to a pontoon. In some open water swimming and higher level triathlon events beach starts are used, and in élite events dive starts are the most common.

Deep Water Floating Start

If you are a weaker swimmer, start towards the back of the pack and to one side. If you are a stronger swimmer, start at the front, but once again to the side, unless this means swimming significantly further to the first buoy.

If you find it easier to breathe to a particular side, then start at the side of the pack which dictates that when you breathe you see other swimmers (as explained in Chapter 3). So if you find it easier to breathe to the right, start to the left of the pack of swimmers, and vice versa.

Lie horizontal in the water and slightly on one side. If you can see the starter from the water, float on the side that allows you to see him most clearly, with your underneath arm out straight in front of you and your other arm down by your side (see Fig. 8.1). To stay comfortably in this position, kick your legs gently and scull slightly with your hands. Practise this, and you will be able to stay stationary and comfortably afloat.

When the gun goes, increase your kicking intensity and pull strongly through with your underneath arm.

Fig. 8.1   Open water swim start position: sculling with one arm out in front, looking towards the starter.

Pontoon Start

If possible, check out the pontoon the day before. Ideally you will find something that you can use as a handhold to keep you comfortably in contact with the pontoon. Hitch your legs up so that your feet are on the pontoon. When the gun goes, push strongly with your feet on the pontoon as you would on the wall in a swimming pool. This will give you a great advantage over all the other swimmers who are just floating next to the pontoon.

Beach Starts

For a beach start you will be required to line up on the land behind a starting line. When the call to start is made you must run into the water and start swimming. It may look like chaos, but in this situation there are some great techniques that you can use to give you an advantage.

Wading

Unless there is a sudden drop-off or shelf on the shore, you will be able to keep running for a distance in the water. This is known as wading, and whilst the water level is below mid-thigh height it is significantly quicker than swimming. However, running in the water can be difficult unless you have become accustomed to it – your top half always seems to be intent on going faster than your bottom half! In addition, with all the other competitors running alongside you the water is not still but swirling about.

To give you more stability, instead of raising your knee up and forwards during the pick-up phase of your running stride, you should rotate your knee inwards. This will cause your foot to rotate outwards, and by moving in this fashion when you come to plant your toes on the ground, your ankle and foot will

Fig. 8.2a–b   Rotate the knee inwards during the running stride to increase stability on the foot plant.

be rotated inwards. In this position you are less likely to twist your ankle on the uneven surface of the seabed, and are thus are more stable.

Once the water becomes higher than mid-thigh, wading takes more effort than dolphin diving (as explained in the following section) or swimming.

Dolphin Diving

When the water becomes too deep to wade efficiently, switch to dolphin diving. Dive

Fig. 8.3a–e   Dolphin diving.

down to the seabed, touch it with your hands, pull your feet forwards and then push up and forwards off the seabed. Once you break the surface, pull your arms backwards under you and then over your head in a butterfly motion. Use the force from this to dive down again and repeat the motion. Use your head angle to control the direction you are travelling in.

Once the water is deeper than approximately waist height it will be faster for you to move into a normal swimming motion. Kick hard, and try to break free from the mêlée behind you.

Dive Starts

Dive starts are rarely demanded in amateur events, but are frequently required in élite events. This will often, though not always, be from a pontoon.

A normal racing dive can be used, though take care not to dive down too deeply: if you do, it can be hard to come up in the mêlée, and another swimmer could easily dive on top of you. Practice makes perfect, so get a few friends together in training, and practise. You can do this in a swimming pool with three or four swimmers diving in next to one another in a normal-width swimming lane. Practising in open water from a pontoon will, of course, give you a much better idea of the real thing – but as always, make sure the water is deep enough to dive into safely.

Exits

There is really only one way to exit from a swim – up a ramp or beach – but the technique to use is significantly different between triathlons and straightforward open water swimming events.

Triathlon

When exiting the water, sight well, using

Fig. 8.4a–h Swim until your hand touches the floor, wade in the shallow water and then run up the bank; whilst running, undo the wetsuit zip and pull the wetsuit down to the waist. Once at your place in transition, pull the wetsuit further down and stamp on it to pull it off and over your ankles and feet.

landmarks on the shore to make sure you are swimming straight towards the exit. Kick a little harder during the last couple of hundred metres to encourage blood to fill your leg muscles so they are ready to carry you into the transition phase and on to the next leg of the race. If this is a sea swim and you are comfortable swimming in waves, you can take full advantage of this and body surf your way into shore: by doing this you can obtain a significant advantage.

Don't stand up until your fingers scrape the ground or exit ramp. Once vertical, use your wading technique to exit the water. Running on sand is challenging because the sand particles trap air between them, meaning that the ground is not solid and can be compressed. In particular, as you strike the sand, the sand particles are compressed together as air is squeezed out. This compression means that less energy is returned to you via rebound, and so you must exert more effort to move forwards. Some studies have found that running on sand requires up to 30 per cent more energy than running on concrete. To increase your efficiency when running on sand, use small quick steps and keep your feet as flat as possible so that your load is spread over a larger surface area.

Unzip your wetsuit whilst running to transition, and pull it down to your waist. Once you are in transition, pull the suit further down in one smooth motion so that it is below your knees, and stamp your way out of it, treading on the body part to hold it down whilst pulling one leg out, then repeat with the other leg. Make sure you keep it in your area of the transition so that it does not get into the way of any other competitor.

Open Water Swimming Event

If completing an open water event you are into your final few seconds of work, so kick as hard as you can while keeping your technique in check and pull strongly.

There is sometimes an overhead board which you are required to hit to get your finish time and position. In this case swim directly under this and simply reach your arm up slightly to tap the board once you are underneath. The race board is usually set up the day before the race, so if possible practise your finish on the course to get a feel for how high the finish board is.

Turning around Buoys

There are different types of buoy that you will need to navigate when swimming: less than 90-degree ('oblique') turns, 90-degree ('right angle') turns, and 90–180-degree ('reflex') turns. In each situation a different type of turn will be the most suitable.

Before we discuss the specific differences of these turns it is important to understand a few points on positioning. If you take the line closest to the buoy you run the risk of being caught in the mêlée: this can slow you down, and can also be quite frightening because you come into contact with other swimmers' arms and legs and will no doubt get knocked about quite a bit. If, however, you take the wide route around the buoy you will have to swim further but will be safely away from the commotion. Beginner swimmers should take the outer route to avoid experiencing the claustrophobic inside line, whilst faster, more experienced swimmers should always try to

Fig. 8.5a–c For a turn less than 90 degrees, swim with your head up and carry out short strokes during the few metres before and after the turn buoy. Shortly after the turn determine your new vantage point and resume normal swimming.

Fig. 8.6a–c For a 90-degree turn, swim with your head up and carry out short strokes during the few metres before and after the turn buoy. Shortly after the turn determine your new vantage point and resume normal swimming.

Fig. 8.7a–d Rotational swim turn: a) with the shoulders level with the buoy, carry out a strong pull with the inside arm

b) flip on to your back;

c) then flip back on to your front;

and d) commence swimming normally, ensuring you incorporate extra sights to determine a new vantage point in the first few strokes after the turn.

take the shortest path around the course and thus should head for the inside line.

Less than 90-degree Turns

These buoys simply require you to slightly alter your direction: you don't need to alter your cadence or technique when swimming around these types of turn. All you will need to do is carry out a few sights close together to obtain your new sighting point, then you are safe to resume your normal sighting pattern for your next point of the course.

90-degree Turns

The best way to tackle a 90-degree turn buoy is to swim normally up to the buoy, but when you come within a few metres of it, raise your head and shorten your stroke. Swim in this fashion around the buoy until you are a few metres clear of it. Whilst swimming in this fashion take the opportunity to get your bearings and determine your route to your next point of the course. Once you have determined this, and are a few metres clear of the turn buoy – and the usual mêlée that surrounds a right-angle turn buoy – it is safe to resume your normal swimming technique.

90–180° Turns

Probably the trickiest buoy to navigate is the 90–180-degree turn buoy. There are really two ways to tackle these: you can swim round the buoy in the same fashion as you navigated the 90-degree turn buoy, although this method is slower than the more technical rotation turn. Effectively you are stopping, turning, and then building up speed in the opposite direction. The rotation turn is best suited to the faster swimmer, but it requires that you have a good line-up to the buoy.

- Swim up to the buoy, and once it is level with your shoulders, carry out one strong pull with your arm closest to the buoy
- Use this force to rotate you on to your back
- Now your inside arm should be above your head, so pull with this arm and rotate about your middle back on to your front so that you are now facing the opposite direction.
- Commence swimming normally, incorporating a couple of sights into your first ten arm strokes to determine and align yourself correctly with a new sighting point

This method maintains some of your momentum and gets you around and away from the buoy in the shortest time possible.

CHAPTER 9

NUTRITION

Good nutrition is important for everyone. However, if you are taking part in a sporting event, then the repercussions of not paying sufficient attention to good nutrition are somewhat greater than those for a more sedentary person. In addition you are using much more energy, and in a different way, and consequently the type of nutrition you need is different.

Nutrition and Performance

It is easy, when you get involved working towards a particular target event, to become obsessed with diet, supplements, what you eat and what you don't. But for most of the time balance is key, and you should only start 'loading' your diet in the last few days before the event. A balanced diet is vital if you are to achieve optimal performance and thus enjoy your event fully. A mix of carbohydrates, protein and healthy fats is necessary to provide the fuel that the body can then use to create and maintain energy.

Carbohydrates are broken down by the body, and the components are used to regulate blood sugar, blood glycogen and muscle glycogen levels, all of which are vital for preventing physical fatigue.

Eating too many fatty foods is commonly known to result in weight gain and diminishing health. However, restricting fat intake too much is also unwise. Your body needs essential fatty acids which can be found in foods such as oily fish and nuts and seeds. Further to this in an event lasting more than an hour, fats can provide up to 75 per cent of the energy used to sustain aerobic output and performance.

Protein is necessary for recovery and for building new tissue, and can also provide energy in particularly long-lasting events.

Hydration

Not only can dehydration affect your performance, it is also extremely dangerous. The bulk of our body's weight is from water, and this level must be maintained. When we participate in sports we lose water in sweat, respiration and the body's metabolic processes. This water is necessary to transport nutrients through the body and to preserve musculoskeletal lubrication, so if it is not sufficiently replaced this can lead to fatigue, muscular pain and ultimately damage to your joints.

The Three Days before the Event

Studies have shown that it is only possible to store enough glycogen in the body to sustain ninety minutes of physical exercise. Consequently, ensuring your glycogen stores are full to the brim on the start line is important to ensure optimal performance in longer distance events such as most open water swimming races and Olympic distance triathlons. This is best done by upping your carbohydrate intake in the three days before your event.

During everyday life it is advisable to consume 5 to 7g of carbohydrate per kilogram of bodyweight. During the three days prior to your event you should increase this to 8 to 10g of carbohydrate per kilogram of bodyweight. So a 70kg person needs to increase their daily intake from between 350 and 490g to between 560 and 700g. It is better to do this by eating little and often than by simply increasing your meal size, because this gives your body a better chance of metabolizing the extra carbohydrate, and will also tend to prevent the lethargy that can easily follow a massive carbohydrate-loaded meal.

Increasing protein intake a small amount will give you a further boost, as protein slows the digestion of carbohydrates, effectively encouraging a slower release of energy. However, it is important not to hugely increase overall calorie intake during these three days.

The Pre-event Meal

It is recommended that you eat three to four hours before the event, as this will allow sufficient time for optimal digestion and energy supply. This meal should provide between 500 and 1,000 calories and should be high in starch, which should ideally be in the form of complex carbohydrates. Suitable foods include breads, cereal, fruits, pasta and vegetables.

Starchy meals should be consumed in this window before an event or training as they are broken down into the building blocks used by the body to release energy more quickly than protein or fats. Starchy foods provide consistent energy and are emptied from the stomach in two to three hours. Fatty or high-fibre or lactose foods should be avoided in a pre-event meal as they take longer to digest than starchy foods. High-sugar foods cause a rapid peak in blood sugar followed by a sudden dip, meaning a decrease in energy. Sugary foods can also dehydrate the body as they draw fluid into the gut for digestion. Other foods that can result in dehydration are those containing caffeine, due to the increased urine production associated with caffeine consumption.

During the period between your pre-event meal and the start of the event, sip on a carb-electrolyte drink every ten to twenty minutes until the start of the event. Caffeine can be included in your pre-event meal, but staying hydrated is vital and thus it is imperative to include water in this meal and to keep a close eye on your hydration levels.

During the Event

When determining your feeding requirements during your event it is important to consider the physiological demands you will be making on your body. From this we can then determine what your body needs to create energy to sustain these demands. Open water swim events require sustained maximal aerobic capacity with a low need for anaerobic power. Due to this your body requires oxygen and carbohydrates in order to have high enough muscle and blood glycogen stores. In order to meet these needs you must optimize your carbohydrate stores and hydration prior to competition, as explained earlier in this chapter. It is then important to sustain carbohydrate delivery and hydration during competition.

By taking on the correct fuel during your event you keep your blood sugar levels high, which means that your glycogen stores are kept in reserve. This in turn prevents fatigue and inhibits cortisol release, which is associated with stress and further fatigue.

It is important to keep in mind that the optimal feeding strategy for each person will vary slightly, and thus guidelines should be implemented in training to determine your specific plan. When practising feeding during training the focus should be placed on what to consume, when and how to do this. Once you have established this, practise missing a few planned feeds in training: this way you see how your body responds to this, and you also give your body the opportunity to adapt to less fuel with the same performance demands.

During a 10km event it is advisable to feed at 5km and 7.5km. At the 5km point taking a liquid meal is best. Gels or solid food will require you to consume liquids separately, and this will take double the time it takes to consume the feed and so too the disruption to your swimming efficiency. Consequently a carbohydrate/electrolyte mix drink is ideal, as you will obtain energy from the carbohydrates, and the liquid will ensure you remain hydrated. You can buy pre-made carbohydrate/electrolyte drink mixes, or you can make your own by combining fresh juices with water and some salt. However, you will need to practise to get the mix right.

The ideal quantities of carbohydrates to take on at your feed stations are 1.2g of carbohydrate per kilogram of bodyweight.

If you are a faster swimmer and arrive at your 7.5km feed station feeling strong, then this feed station is optional. You will probably have 25 minutes or less of swimming left to do, and as long as you fed at your 5km feed station you should have enough energy to finish the race strongly. However, if you have the time to feed here – that is, you are not jostling for positions or trying to dip under a time – then it is still advisable to take on calories at this point.

Once again, a carbohydrate/electrolyte drink mix is ideal. Caffeine is useful to include in your feed at this point of the event, but must be practised in training as tolerance levels, and response times vary greatly between individuals.

If you missed your 5km feeding station, are not feeling strong, or are a slower swimmer and so probably have 35 minutes or more left of swimming to do, then the 7.5km feed station is a must.

It is not necessary to feed during an Olympic distance triathlon as the swim should take only around 20 to 30 minutes, but you will need to feed on the bike leg. This is best achieved by attaching gel packs to the bike with tape.

HOW TO FEED

It is important to establish a plan for the feeder, and to practise this plan with your feeder as much as is possible. When you reach your feeding station, swim close enough to your feeder to be handed a cup with your feed in. If this is not possible then you must practise taking the cup or feeding pack from the feeding pole. Stay horizontal whilst feeding, and consume the entire feed.

Recovery

Making nutrition a priority immediately after training or an event is important for your recovery and to ensure you are ready to go for your next training session or event. It is difficult to meet energy and fluid needs during physical activity. Firstly it is difficult to consume liquids or foods whilst training or competing, and what you do manage to consume is not well metabolized by your body because your blood is directed away from your digestive organs to your working muscles. Consequently refuelling post training and post event is essential. Eating a high sodium, well balanced meal – that is, a meal containing a mix of carbohydrates, fats and protein – within 30 minutes of completion is ideal. Protein synthesis is optimal during this window, and carbohydrates are needed to restore muscle and blood glycogen stores. Foods such as bananas, apples or whole-grain bagels are ideal.

IRON

Lack of iron can reduce aerobic capacity and impair performance. However, iron is a greedy supplement and will minimize absorption of other supplements taken. Because of this it is important to manage your normal diet to include a good level of iron-rich foods: this can be done by eating red meat, dark leafy greens, whole grains and legumes. Only take supplements as a last resort, and never overload on iron supplementation.

Nutrition and Our Mood

It is fairly well accepted that eating poorly can see our waistlines expand and our energy dwindle or become erratic. However, it is less well recognized that what we eat can significantly affect our mood. This is due to a chemical called serotonin, and since our mood will affect our performance and how we tackle our training, it is an important fact to consider.

What is Serotonin?

Serotonin is a neurotransmitter. Neurotransmitters are responsible for passing messages across nerve synapses. Serotonin works with other transmitters and changes the neuron's responses to specific signals: specifically, its job is to regulate the intensity of the signals it transmits. Think of this a little like a volume control on a radio, which acts to make signals fainter or louder.

Serotonin is used all over the body, and thus its levels in our body can radically alter a wide range of our behaviours. In particular exceedingly high levels of serotonin have been shown to have a sedative effect. But within the 'normal' range, low levels of serotonin cause us to be depressed, whereas high levels see us happier. Consequently, while we want to aim for a high level of serotonin intake, it can be disastrous to overdo it.

Serotonin is simply referred to as a mood neurotransmitter and is often thought to exist mainly in the brain. However, surprisingly, between 80 and 90 per cent of the body's serotonin is found in the gut. Our stomachs use a huge amount of serotonin each day, and consequently it is necessary for us to eat a serotonin-rich diet to ensure that levels are kept balanced. Foods known to boost serotonin levels include chicken, fish, tomatoes, turkey and walnuts.

In order for your body to metabolize these foods and release serotonin it is necessary to eat a small amount of high carbohydrate foods. However, white flour and sugary carbohydrate should be avoided as these boost serotonin levels in the short term, but in the long term result in unstable serotonin and energy levels. Further to this, eating protein prior to carbohydrates has been shown to stop spikes in serotonin level from occurring.

CHAPTER 10

BASIC TRAINING PROGRAMMES

When entering into a new sport it is easy to envisage the rosy glow of successfully achieving your goal – perhaps you see yourself crossing the finish line as if in slow motion to the accompaniment of *Chariots of Fire*. However, a moment's reflection is enough for us to realize that nothing valuable can be achieved in sport without the appropriate training.

One of the issues with open water swimming is that virtually every race is an endurance event, so there really is no escaping the long hours of focused training which are required to build your body's stamina to the necessary level. Professional élite athletes will normally dedicate up to thirty hours a week to training during the season. But the good news is that, if you do the hours, you will get there. In other words, the tunnel may be long, but there is always a light at the end of it.

Proper training should be tailored to the specific needs and development progress of the individual athlete, and it is beyond the scope of this book to describe in detail the principles of training programme design. However, if you follow the general drift of the following sample programmes you should put yourself in a good position to tackle your next race.

Although the programmes below are set out in such a way as to be interesting and fun, some of the sessions are relatively long and at times motivation can hit rock bottom. Setting a series of goals en route to achieving your big season goal will keep you pushing forwards. Goals should be SMART, which is the acronym for the following guidelines:

Specific – It is important that the goal outlines exactly what will be achieved and by whom.

Measurable – This term highlights the fact that you must be able to determine whether you have achieved your goal or not. It also ensures that you can track your progress towards achieving your goal, which will thus keep you motivated.

Achievable – A goal may stretch you, but it must not be unrealistic. It is also important that the goal is not too easy and below your level of performance.

Relevant – Is it the right time to set the goal, and is it a worthwhile goal for you?

Time bounded – Having a committed deadline within which to achieve your goal will help you to focus your attention, and will ensure that you achieve the goal in an efficient time.

10km Open Water Swim

Ten kilometres is a long way, but with the help of this programme not only will you complete the distance, but you will also enjoy your experience. Your aim is to carry out three sessions per week, which will focus on building endurance, improving your technical skills, and increasing sustainable speed.

You should carry out one long swim per week, which ideally will be in the open water. If this is not possible, however, try to simulate open water swimming by swimming without touching the ends of the pool; this plan will take you from three months to the event up to race day. In week one, your long swim should be 3km, and this should be increased by 500m each week so that two weeks before the race you complete a 7.5km swim. With one week to go to the event, carry out a 5km swim as part of your taper. During these swims practise feeding, but feed no more than every 30 minutes.

The second of the three sessions each week should focus on intervals to build speed and fitness. During these sessions the overall distance should be kept long, but intervals should be incorporated. Two example sessions are below:

Session 1
500m swim, 400m pull paddle band buoy (ppbb), 300m individual medley (IM), 200m kick, 100m backstroke 3 × 1,500m as:
- 500m swim, 500m pull buoy only, 500m paddles only
- 3 × (200m hard, 300m easy)
- (50m hard, 150m easy, 100m hard, 100m easy, 150m hard, 50m easy, 200m hard, 50m easy, 150m hard, 100m easy, 100m hard, 150m easy, 50m hard, 100m easy)
300m warm-down

Session 2
3 × (400m swim, 200m IM).
6 × 400m as two swim race pace, two IM, two swim race pace, two ppbb

2 × (4 × 50m, 200m) with paddles and fins on, aiming the summation of the 50m times to equal the 200m time. Pace = hard.

10 × 50m with lots of rest starting with nine breaths per 50m and decreasing by one each length: aim to get to 0, but stop at the number you progress to and stay there or try to decrease.
200m warm-down.

The third session in the week should focus on a mix of building strength and improving swimming technique. The total distance covered during these sessions will be shorter than that in the other two sessions. During these sessions it is important to work on drills that concentrate on your specific stroke deficiencies. For example, the rotation drill will be useful for a swimmer who swims too flat in the water, whilst the opposition drill will help swimmers with timing issues (see the photos below for demonstrations of these two drills). Using paddles, band, pull buoy, drag shorts, sponges and towels around your band are all ways of increasing resistance and thus helping you to build strength whilst swimming and training for your event with specificity.

Triathlon

Olympic Distance 1,500m
Below there are two programmes set out, one for a complete beginner whose aim is simply to complete the distance, and the other for a more advanced athlete whose goal is to be competitive over the distance.

As a novice, you need to gradually build up the distance you swim so that you are confident you can complete the 1,500m. Remember you will have the bike and run to contend with afterwards, so it is important that you

Fig. 10.1a–c   Rotation drill: a) carry out six kicks whilst on your side, pull through and rotate to the other side, carry out six kicks in this position, repeat; then b) pull through with the left arm as the right leg kicks down; c) repeat with the right arm and the left leg.

are able to complete the swim section with some energy left in the tank.

As an advanced swimmer you need to work on the different areas of your fitness to ensure that you have a solid base. Some sessions are to be completed aerobi-cally, others at race pace or maximal sprint speed. Further to this, any inefficiencies in technique should be ironed out, and physical strength needs to be built up. All these aspects are taken care of in the protocol below.

Table 2   Sample training programme

	Beginner	Advanced
Week 1:	**Swim 1:** 16 × 25m alternating front crawl (fc), kick, pull, another stroke than front crawl 10 sec rest between each 25m **Swim 2:** 8 × 25m fc 10sec rest between, 8 × 25m pull fc 10sec rest between, 8 × 25m as (25m sculling with pull buoy, 25m swim scull once in each of the three catch positions front under chest and by thigh on the final 25m scull move gradually through the three positions i.e. spend approximately 8m in each position), 8 × 25m alternating fc and one other stroke	**Swim 1:** 5 × 200m swim warm-up as swim, pull, kick, pull, swim *Main set (at race pace):* 50m 10sec rest, 100m 15sec rest, 150m 25sec rest 200m 30sec rest, 200m 30sec rest, 150m 25sec rest, 100m 20sec rest, 50m 200m warm-down **Swim 2:** 400m swim, 300m pull paddles buoy band (ppbb), 200m kick, 100m swim, 4 × 50m as 15m hard, 35m easy *Main set:* 8 × 50m as fast as you can go (MAX MAX MAX) off 90sec: that is, your swimming and rest time for each 50m should add up to 90sec 400m warm-down **Swim 3:** 20 × 100m off the same time approximately 10sec rest: this should be at your aimed race pace, 200m swim-down, 4 × 50m as 15m hard, 35m easy **Swim 4:** (optional) 500m swim, 400m ppbb, 300m kick, 200m IM, 100m swim
Week 2:	**Swim 1:** 8 × 25m alternating fc and another stroke 10sec rest between, 4 × 100m alternating fc and pull 8 × 25m scull to swim (as explained in week 1) **Swim 2:** 100m swim warm-up, 2 × 50m fast 20sec rest between, 2 × 100m easy 15sec rest between, 200m fast, 200m easy swim warm down	**Swim 1:** 5 × 200m swim warm-up as swim, pull, kick, pull, swim *Main set (at race pace):* 50m 10sec rest, 100m 15sec rest, 150m 25sec rest; 200m 30sec rest, 200m 30sec rest, 150m 25sec rest, 100m 20sec rest, 50m 10sec rest, 50m 10sec rest, 100m 15 sec rest, 150m 25sec rest 200m 30sec rest 200m warm-down **Swim 2:** 400m swim, 300m ppbb, 200m kick, 100m swim, 4 × 50m as 15m hard, 35m easy *Main set:* 3 × 200m MAX MAX MAX 3min rest between 400m warm-down **Swim 3:** 30 × 100m off the same time approximately 10sec rest: this should be at your aimed race pace, 200m swim-down, 4 × 50m as 15m hard, 35m easy **Swim 4:** (optional) 500m swim, 400m ppbb, 300m kick, 200m IM, 100m swim

BASIC TRAINING PROGRAMMES

	Beginner	**Advanced**

Week 3: | **Swim 1:** Continuous swim for 20min
Swim 2: 100m swim warm-up, 8 × 25m as 25m scull 25m swim, 3 × 200m as 50m fast, 50m easy, 30sec rest between each 200, 100m swim-down

Swim 1: 5 × 200m swim warm-up as swim, pull, kick, pull, swim
Main set (at race pace):
150m 25sec rest 200m 30sec rest, 200m 30sec
2 × (50m 10sec rest, 100m 15sec rest,
100m 20sec rest, 50m 10sec rest)
200m warm-down
Swim 2: 400m swim, 300m ppbb, 200m kick, 100m swim, 4 × 50m as 15m hard, 35m easy
Main set: 8 × 50m MAX MAX MAX off 90sec
400m warm-down
Swim 3: 40 × 100m off the same time approximately 10sec rest: this should be at your aimed race pace, 200m swim-down,
4 × 50m as 15m hard, 35m easy.
Swim 4: (optional) 500m swim, 400m ppbb, 300m kick, 200m IM, 100m swim

Week 4: **Easy week**
Swim 1: 20 × 25m alternating (swim, pull, kick, scull) 10sec rest between each 25m
Swim 2: 200m swim, 200m pull, 8 × 25m scull to swim, 200m swim

Easy week:
Swim 1: 5 [x] 200m as swim, pull, kick, pull, swim
Main set: (100m, 200m, 300m, 400m, 400m, 300m, 200m, 100m) all off same base time, i.e. if off 90 for 100m 200m is off 3min, etc. Pace = aerobic.
200m warm-down
Swim 2: 4 × 400m as swim, 4 × (50m fly, 50m swim), 4 × (50m drill of your choice, 50m swim), 4 × (50m kick, 50m pull)
800m continuous as 50m hard, 150m easy, 100m hard, 100m easy, 150m hard, 50m easy, 200m hard
200m warm-down
Swim 3: (optional) 12 [x] 200m as 4 swim, 4 ppbb, 4 IM, 4 swim 15sec rest between

Week 5: **Swim 1:** Continuous swim for 25min
Swim 2: 100m warm-up, 5 × 100m alternating easy/hard 15sec rest between, 100m easy, 5 × 100m alternating easy/hard 15sec rest between, 100m warm-down

Swim 1: 5 × 200m swim warm-up as swim, pull, kick, pull, swim
Main set (at race pace):
2 × (50m 10sec rest, 100m 15sec rest, 150m 25sec rest 200m 30 ec rest, 200m 30sec rest, 150m 25sec rest, 100m 20sec rest, 50m 10sec rest)
With paddles and mini fins on:
3 × (2 × 50m, 100m hard aiming to double 50m time for the 100m 15sec rest between)
200m warm-down
Swim 2: 400m swim, 300m ppbb, 200m kick, 100m swim, 4 × 50m as 15m hard, 35m easy
Main set: 5 × 200m MAX MAX MAX 3min rest between
400m warm-down

Beginner	Advanced
	Swim 3: 50 × 100m off the same time approximately 10sec rest: this should be at your aimed race pace, 200m swim-down, 4 × 50m as 15m hard, 35m easy
	Swim 4: (optional) 500m swim, 400m ppbb, 300m kick, 200m IM, 100m swim
Week 6: **Race Week**	**Race Week**
Swim 1: 100m warm up, 100m hard, 8 × 25m as scull to swim, 8 × 50m alternating easy/hard 5sec rest, 100m easy, 4 × 50m as 15m hard 35m easy 30sec rest, 100m easy. Practise getting wetsuit off if it is a wetsuit swim	**Swim 1:** 5 × 200m as swim, pull, kick, pull, swim 12 × 50m as every third hard 10sec rest, 8 × 50m as every second hard 15sec rest, 4 × 50m as every one hard 20sec rest. 300m warm-down finishing with 4 [x] 50m as 15m hard 35m easy
RACE DAY!	**Swim 2:** 750–1,000m continuous including 8 × 15m fast swimming (on the course if possible). Practise starts and exits
	Swim 3: (optional) 200m swim, 2 × (100m race pace, 4 × 50m race pace) 200m swim-down
	RACE DAY!

Core Stability Programme

In order to achieve an effective swimming stroke, forces need to be transferred diagonally across the body through the core. If this is to be achieved efficiently, a good level of core stability and strength endurance is necessary.

To understand this more effectively it can be useful to consider the analogy of a swimmer to a piece of spaghetti. A swimmer with a weak core may be likened to cooked spaghetti, in that with a weak core he is floppy in the water and cannot be propelled effectively through it: he or she simply flops around, and if left too long, will eventually sink. On the other hand a swimmer with a strong, tenacious core can be compared to uncooked spaghetti, which can be pushed through the water easily. So it can be seen that core stability is vital to achieve efficient swimming.

As explained in Chapter 11, which deals with possible injuries and how to handle them, back injuries are one of the more common swimming injuries. Technical errors can lead to back pain in swimmers, although the specific etiology for most back injuries is unknown. Recent scientific advances have demonstrated that spinal instability is a common cause of back pain. Spinal stability is the capability of the stabilizing system of the spine to maintain segments of the spine within their physiological limits. In an unstable spine, larger motions than the body is capable of tolerating are present between individual vertebrae. These motions cause either compressive or tensile deformation of the associated soft tissue structures, such as ligaments, joint capsules, cartilaginous end-plates or annular fibres.

In either situation, excessive forces can result in pathophysiological changes that may result in pain. It has been shown that increasing local core muscle activity is effective at increasing passive joint stiffness and thus improving spinal stability. In particular, increased activity of the *transverse abdominus* (TA) and *lumbar multifdii* (MF) muscles have been associated with improved spinal stability.

It is generally accepted that there are two distinct muscular systems that make up the core and work in synergy to stabilize the spine. The TA and MF are both part of the 'local' system, whilst the global system contains muscles such as the rectus abdominus (RA), which acts to flex the spine. All muscles in the global system are muscles which work to move the spine, whist all muscles in the local system have their origin or insertion at a vertebra. Active treatment for back pain has previously focused on strengthening the RA, but this has been seen to

Table 3   Sample core stability programme

Exercise	Sets and reps of hold duration	Description
Prone plank	Up to 2min × 3	Lie face down on the floor, your feet shoulder-width apart, and place your hands under your shoulders. Lift yourself up, keep your arms straight but do not lock your elbows. Look down towards the floor and slightly forwards, your shoulder blades neutrally protracted. See Fig. 10.2.
Side plank	45–60sec each side × 3	Lie on your side, place one foot in front of the other side on contacting the floor. Place both hands on the floor and push yourself up. Remove your upper hand from the floor and place it on your side. Keep your body in a straight line and don't let your hip lag down. See Fig. 10.3.
Swimming	30 each side × 3	Lie prone on your front, head down; lift one arm and the opposite leg off the floor approximately 5cm, lower and repeat other side. Conduct this slowly and in a controlled manner. See Fig. 10.4.
TA	5 each side × 3	Lie on your back, find your hip bones and come in approximately 2cm and down 1cm. Cough, and you will feel the muscle under your fingers contract. Your aim is to contract this muscle whilst breathing normally. To contract the muscle, act as if you are trying to stop peeing or suck your belly button into your spine. Once you have mastered this, bend your knees up, feet on the floor. Breathe in, and whilst you breathe out, lift one leg up off the floor. Breathe in with the leg in this position, and when you breathe out again, float the leg out straight, breathe in, and whilst you breathe out, bend the knee back in, then finally breathe in, and whilst you breathe in, float your leg back down. Repeat with the other leg. This is one repetition. See Fig. 10.5a–c..

Fig. 10.2 Prone plank: the feet should be shoulder-width apart, hands under the shoulders, arms straight, the shoulder blades neutrally protracted looking forwards and down.

Fig. 10.3 Side plank: one foot in front of the other, hand under the shoulder, the body held in a straight line.

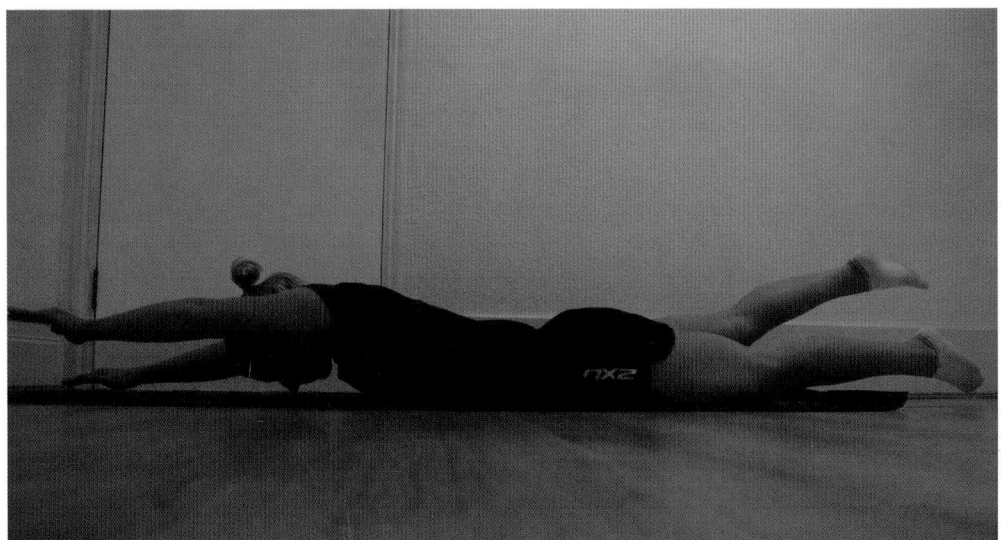

Fig. 10.4   Swimming drill: lying prone, lift one arm and the opposite leg approximately 5cm off the ground; then lower, and repeat with the opposite arm and leg.

Fig. 10.5a–c   Transverse abdominus work. Note that the legs only move on the 'out' breath, and the transverse abdominus must remain activated.

be ineffective. Similarly the majority of fitness programmes overemphasize the RA. This results in an imbalance between the two systems, which has been seen to result in injurious movement patterns leading to compensatory motions and finally back pain.

Bearing all this in mind, the importance of including a properly constructed core stabilizing programme into your training week can be seen.

The TA and MF are both made up predominantly of type I tonic muscle fibres. Any lengthening of these fibres can weaken them, so exercises that target them should allow either no movement, or very small controlled movements. In particular any exercises that target these muscles should allow no movement through the spine or pelvis. That is, no sagging is permitted. A suitable

programme is outlined earlier in this chapter in Table 3, and should be carried out two to three times a week. The exercises are either stationary holds, or should be carried out slowly and in a controlled manner.

Stretching Protocol

As will be discussed in Chapter 11, common upper body injuries in swimmers are due to muscular imbalances about the shoulder, and repetitive use. These factors have been shown to result in stretching of the anteroinferior capsuloligamentous structures. Collectively this results in shoulder instability, which can result in pain and further injury. Consequently no anterior capsular stretches should be carried out, only poste-

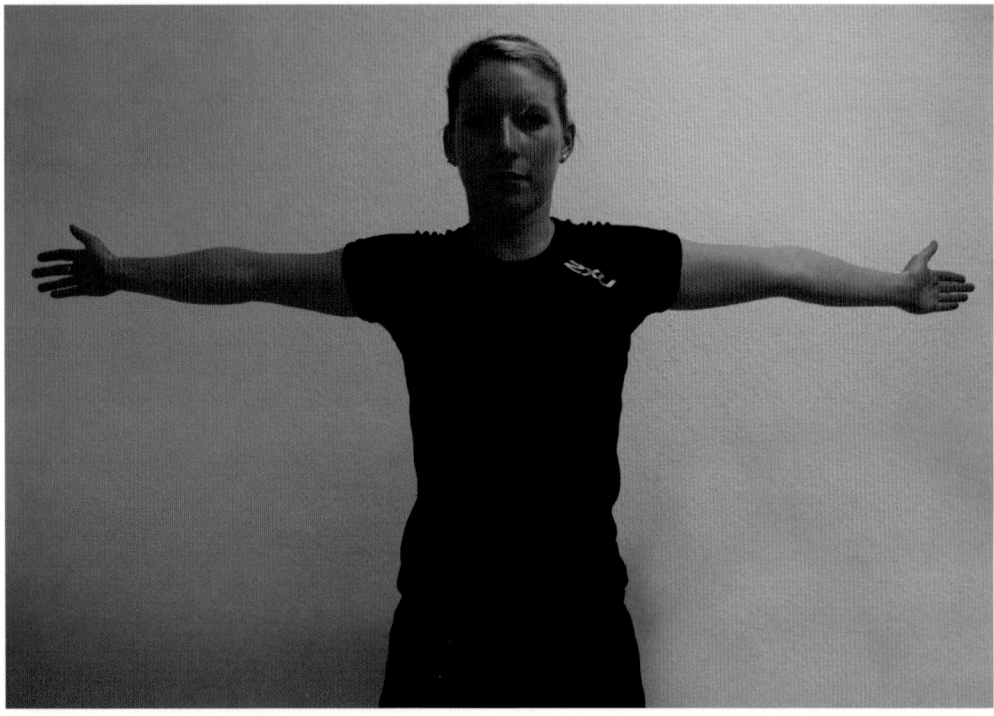

Fig. 10.6a–b   Dynamic shoulder warm-up stretch – 1.

rior stretches. Stretching should be used to allow the internal shoulder rotators and chest muscles to lengthen and thus rebalance the forces that couple about the shoulder joint.

There is a great deal of controversy surrounding static stretching. It is advisable to err on the side of caution, and as a consequence no static stretching should be carried out as part of a warm-up prior to other exercise. However, it is generally accepted that it is safe to include dynamic stretching as part of a warm-up. See below for a few upper body stretches that are useful to include in your weekly training programme:

Warm-up stretch I

This is a dynamic stretch so you should keep moving throughout:

- Lift up your arms and extend them horizontally on each side of your body with the palms facing forwards
- Move them in horizontally across your body, crossing one over the other
- Repeat for about 30sec

Warm-up stretch 2

This is also a dynamic stretch so you should keep moving throughout:

- This stretch is the same as stretch one, but only one arm moves at a time
- Start with your left arm horizontally out to your side with the palm facing forwards
- Swing it in across your body
- Swing it out horizontally, and repeat, alternating one arm, then the other, for 30sec

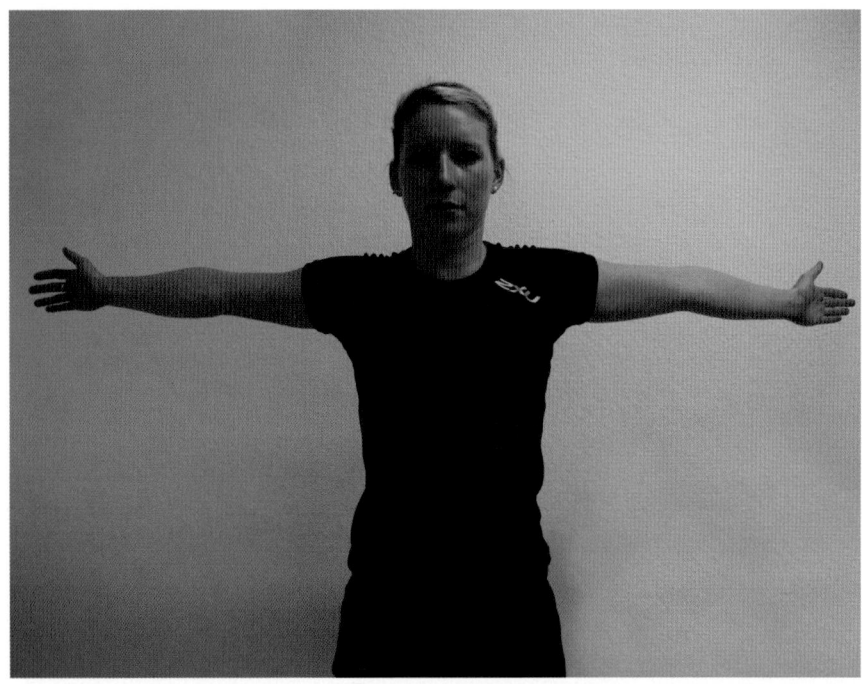

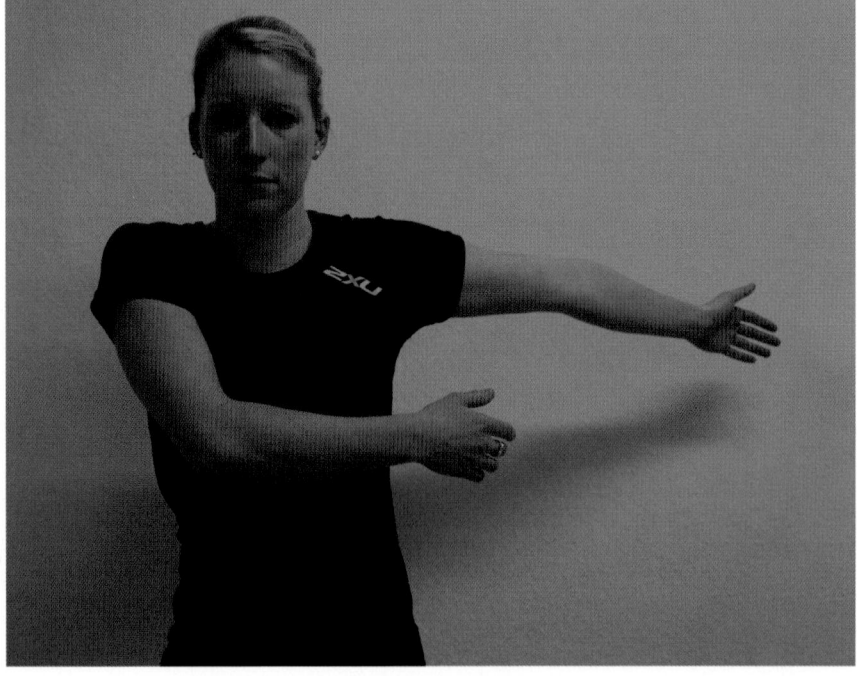

Fig. 10.7a–b Dynamic shoulder warm-up stretch – 2.

Fig. 10.8   Static warm-down stretch – 3.

Warm-up stretch 3

This is also a dynamic stretch so you should keep moving throughout:

- Lean over forwards and let your arms hang down
- Swing your arm in small controlled circles
- Alternate the arms and repeat for two to three sets of 30sec on each arm

Warm-down stretch 1

This is a static stretch so you should keep stationary throughout:

- Stand upright
- Lift your arms above your head, then bend to one side until you feel a stretch down the other side of your body
- Hold this position for 30sec, then repeat on the opposite side

Warm-down stretch 2

This again is a dynamic stretch so you should keep moving throughout:

- Lie on your back, bend your knees up, and hold them, in this position, close in to your chest
- Rock from side to side in small controlled movements, which you will feel massaging your spine
- Continue for 30sec

Fig. 10.9   Dynamic warm-down stretch.

69

CHAPTER 11

POSSIBLE INJURIES AND THEIR MANAGEMENT

Swimming is a non-weight-bearing sport, and so the chances of injury are relatively low when compared to those associated with weight-bearing sports such as running or jumping. However, as with all activities, there is still some risk of injury. Overload is a key component of swimming training, as indicated in Chapter 10, and is the most common cause of swimming-related injury. The most prevalent swimming injuries, and how to avoid them and recover from them, are discussed below.

Medical science in the area of sports-related injury has progressed enormously over the last ten to twenty years, due mainly to the amount of money dedicated to élite professional sports. As a consequence our understanding of these injuries, how to avoid them and how to treat them, has developed accordingly. Much of what follows may seem overly technical, but is there for those of you who want to understand the medical background (refer to the Glossary at the end of the book for an explanation of some of the terms). But if you are only interested in the what, rather than the why, simply ignore the lengthy Latin names.

The Most Common Overload Swimming Injuries

The open water swimmer is at lower risk of

developing an overload injury than a pool-based swimmer. Pool swimming involves a high number of repetitions of the same movements, and so the tissues involved with the motions that make up the swimming stroke are repeatedly loaded. If the overload is too high, either due to swimming volume or to a dysfunction in your stroke, the associated tissues do not have sufficient time to recover and begin to gradually break down. This breakdown results in pain and dysfunction and ultimately injury.

When swimming in open water, various factors such as currents, waves and wind come into play. Further to this, rough water and pack swimming often call for changes in stroke pattern and speed in order to go around buoys, stay with the pack, or overtake other swimmers. These changes and altered demands result in an increased resistance. Rather than just making swimming feel more difficult, these factors cause an increased demand on the stabilizing muscles of the shoulder complex (including the levator scapulae, lower trapezius, rhomboids, rotator cuff and serratus anterior), and strengthening and improving the endurance capabilities of these stabilizing muscles is necessary in order to decrease the risk of shoulder injury in swimmers. Consequently many of the areas that physiotherapists work on with pool swimmers to prevent injury are taken care of when open water swimming whilst training with specificity. Moreover the changes in pace, and therefore the changes in energy demand, challenge the body's various energy systems, meaning that aspects of physiology that are difficult to access when training in the pool are utilized.

Nevertheless, as an open water swimmer you are still at some risk of developing an injury: most commonly this is in the shoulder and back, although there is also some risk of injury to the knee, and cramps are a hazard.

Swimmer's Shoulder

The Injury
Swimmer's shoulder is the most common injury in swimmers. Put simply, excessive repeated use of the shoulder in the swim stroke causes wear and strain, which in turn results in damage and pain. But in scientific terms, swimmer's shoulder is the accepted term used to describe shoulder pain that involves tendinopathy of the rotator cuff (specifically the supraspinatus and long head of biceps), and is part of the impingement syndrome complex. Swimmer's shoulder is a combination of three pathologies: instability, impingement and tendinopathy.

We will now look at the causes of swimmer's shoulder in order to understand why the elements of the rehabilitation programme outlined later on in the chapter are necessary. Stroke length is beneficial to swimming speed and efficiency. Consequently, some shoulder instability can be seen to be favourable in swimmers, as it results in achieving a longer swimming stroke. In addition, high levels of swimming result in shoulder instability, as the repetitive overhead movement causes stretching of the stabilizing structures of the shoulder. Thus it can be seen that

some instability is beneficial to swimming performance, and is created by the necessary training.

Towards the end of the shoulder's range the dynamic stabilizers – in particular the rotator cuff muscles – must work to stabilize the shoulder complex and stop impingement occurring. Muscles work in pairs (one muscle relaxing whilst the other contracts) to create movement. With a large range of shoulder movement the rotator cuff muscles are required to work in awkward positions. At the end of range of movement in an unstable shoulder one muscle is overstretched and so there is insufficient overlap of the actin and myosin (see Glossary), whilst the other is under-stretched and so there is less potential for shortening and translation of the sarcomere. Both of these factors are associated with lower maximal producible tension, meaning the dynamic stabilizers of the shoulder need to be strong to effectively stabilize the shoulder in this position.

Consequently the degree of instability snowballs, and can progress to impingement of the rotator cuff muscles (most commonly the supraspinatus and long head of biceps), resulting in tendinopathy of the affected muscles.

In addition to this, the repetitive motion of swimming has been shown to cause an imbalance in a swimmer's muscularity about the shoulder, with strong internal rotators of the humerus (specifically the pectoralis major and latissimus dorsi) and weak scapula stabilizers and external rotators of the humerus (specifically the middle trapezius, rhomboids, serratus anterior, infraspinatus, posterior deltoid and teres minor). This imbalance results in an abnormal force couple about the shoulder complex, and dysfunctional scapulothoracic motion, and has been significantly linked to shoulder pain.

Table 4   Overload injuries

Demand	Effect	Rehabilitation Focus
Range of movement (ROM)	Rotator cuff (RTC) muscles must work at undesirable lengths	Strengthen RTC muscles
Muscle imbalance	Weak scapular retractors, stabilizers and external rotators	Must strengthen these to address imbalance
Muscle fatigue	Long training sessions result in decreased stability throughout session	Endurance of RTC and scapular stabilizing muscles required

Finally, endurance has been seen to increase swimming performance, and long training sessions are therefore a requirement for competitive open water swimmers. The rotator cuff and scapular stabilizing muscles are active during the entire swimming stroke cycle, resulting in them being at a higher risk of fatigue. These muscles are responsible for dynamically stabilizing the shoulder complex, which during long training sessions

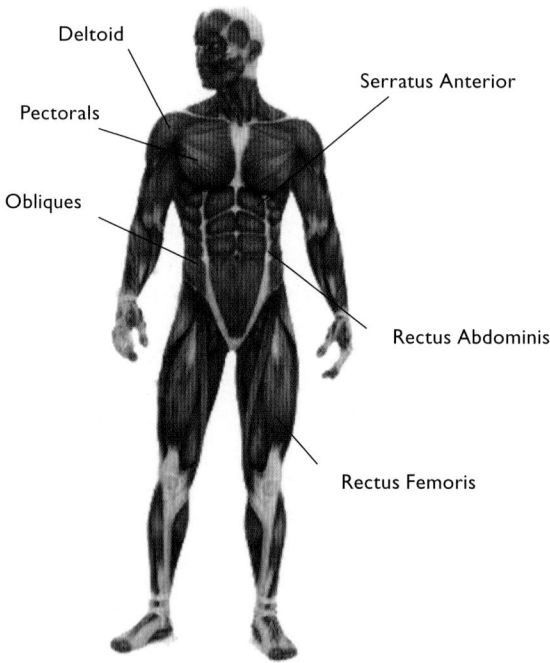

Deltoid

Pectorals

Obliques

Serratus Anterior

Rectus Abdominis

Rectus Femoris

Fig. 11.1

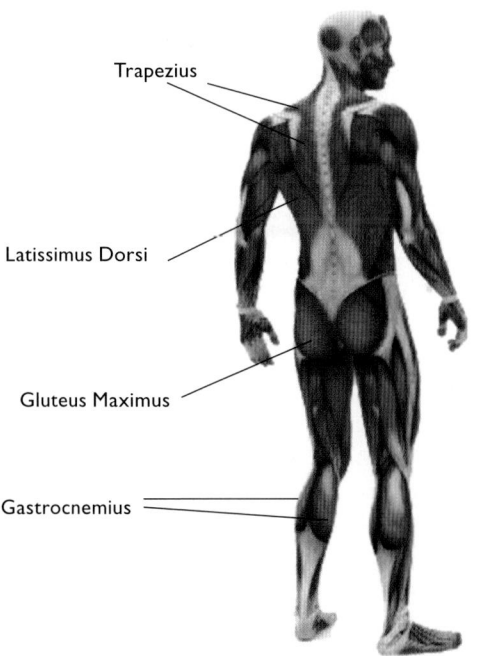

Fig. 11.2

will become gradually less stable, resulting in a higher risk of impingement. The table below links the demands of swimming, the effects of these demands in relation to injury and the risk of injury, and the associated rehabilitation focus.

Rehabilitation

The initial treatment of swimmer's shoulder should focus on the reduction of pain and inflammation. Suggested modalities to do so include rest (in particular the avoidance of aggravating factors such as motion in the impingement zone above 90 degrees of shoulder abduction); ice; massage (initially above the area of pain); ultrasound; and transcutaneous nerve stimulation. As pain decreases and the pain-free range of motion

increases, progress can be made to focus on restoring the 'normal' range of motion. Anterior capsule stretches such as those shown in Fig. 11.3a–b should be avoided, whilst posterior capsules (see Fig. 11.4) are advised.

As pain-free range of motion is increased back to a good level, focus should be placed on strengthening. Muscular balance must be restored. This is achieved by strengthening the external rotators (namely the teres minor and infraspinatus) and the scapular stabilizers (namely the middle trapezius, rhomboids and serratus anterior). Isotonic (the muscle contracts but no movement occurs) exercises are used initially to strengthen the muscles. The force of the contractions should be 20 per cent that of possible maximum force, and contrac-

73

Fig. 11.3a–b Anterior shoulder capsule stretch.

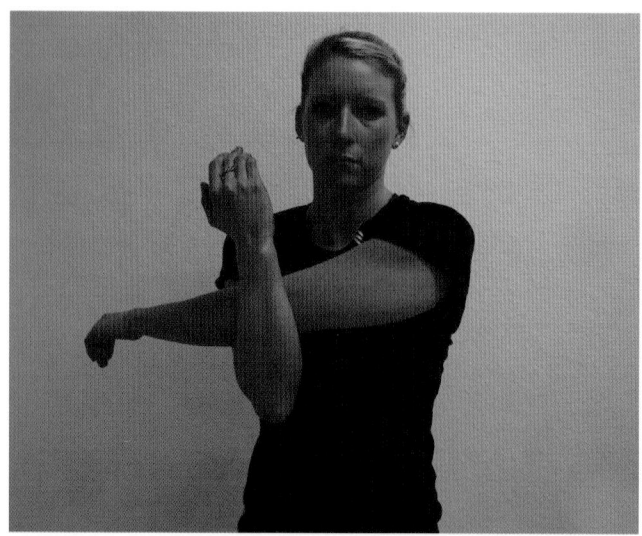

Fig. 11.4 Posterior shoulder capsule stretch.

Table 5   Rehabilitation exercises – 1

	Early:	Intermediate:	Late:
	✓ Shoulder hot and puffy ✓ FULL ROM painful	✓ Full active pain free ROM ✓ Stength imbalances	✓ Strength imbalances remain but are minor ✓ Stroke deficiencies
Goals	Decrease pain and imflammation Restore normal joint and capsular motion	Restore muscular balance and normal capsular motion	Return to sport in full pain-free motion and strength
ROM	Use wooden bar to work pain-free internal and external rotation and flexion and extension	None	None
Manual therapy	Posterior capsule stretches	Continue posterior capsule stretches	Continue if imbalances remain
Strengthening	Isometric shoulder abduction and external rotation. Isometric flexion and extension should be carried out with secondary importance	Add isotonic shoulder abduction and external rotation exercises. Also the Serratus anterior side-lying external rotation and standing row (shoulder retraction) exercises	Continue strengthening programme focusing on external rotators (namely the teres minor and infraspinatus) and the scapular stabilizers (namely the middle trapezius; rhomboids and serratus anterior). Isotonic upper extremity strengthening machines to be used
Proprioceptive	Wall ball alphabets	Continue wall alphabets with smaller ball and eyes closed	None
Restrictions	In water: leg kick only On land: no overhead movements or anterior capsule stretches	In water: leg kick and drills with motion only under the horizontal plane On land: No overhead activity	None

tions should be held for 6–10 seconds. The exercises to be carried at this stage of rehabilitation are shown in the Table 5.

Once three sets of fifteen repetitions of an exercise can be completed without causing pain (and not before), the exercise can be progressed to isometric (the muscles are worked and movement occurs). Initially a stretch cord should be used with its normal resistance, and finally weights added to increase resistance. The resistance should only be increased once three sets of fifteen repetitions of an exercise can be carried out without causing pain.

Fig. 11.5a–b *Isotonic shoulder abduction exercise.*

Fig. 11.6a–b *Isotonic external rotation exercise.*

 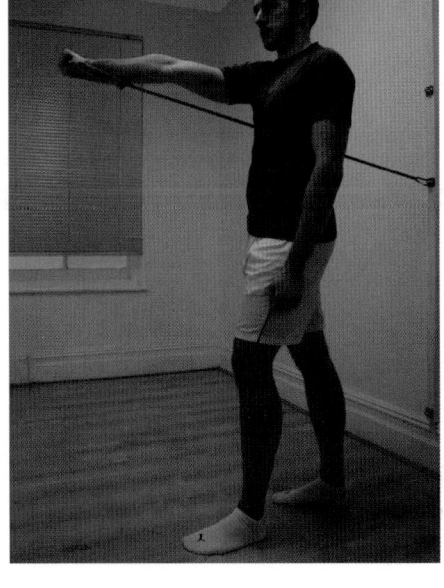

Fig. 11.7a–b   Serratus anterior exercise.

Back Injuries

One cause of back pain in swimmers is the repetitive stress during tumble turns. As an open water swimmer you avoid this stress. However, the arching required during sighting, and the possibility of a poor head position in the water, can also place a great deal of strain on the back, which can result in injury. The most prevalent back injuries seen in the swimmer include spondylolysis, spondylolisthesis and Scheurmann's kyphosis (see Glossary).

Scheurmann's kyphosis is the term used to describe adolescent 'swimmer's back', which occurs due to repetitive flexion of the thoracic spine. This injury is most common in butterfly swimmers, and so open water swimmers generally have a decreased risk of developing this injury. However, the arching required for sighting if carried out incorrectly can predispose adolescent open water swimmers to this injury.

Rehabilitation
Recovery includes avoiding diving and tumble turns. Core stability work is beneficial, with particular focus placed on transverse abdominal function and endurance. (See the core protocol set out in Chapter 10.) Further to this, improving hamstring flexibility is necessary.

Knee Injuries

As an open water swimmer it is likely that you will be swimming front crawl, but it is important to be aware of the different injury risks that other strokes present. For example, there is an increased risk of knee and hip injury when swimming breast-

Fig. 11.8a–b   External rotation lying on your side.

Table 6   Rehabilitation exercises – 2

	Early:	Intemediate:	Late:
	✓ Some pain weight-bearing ✓ Knee hot and puffy	✓ Full pain free weight-bearing ✓ Some loss of strength remains	✓ Full pain-free ROM and weight-bearing ✓ Minor strength deficits remain
Goals	Reduce pain and swelling Maintain ROM Prevent quadriceps atrophy	Increase ROM Restore strength Increase function	Resolve remaining strength deficits Prepare for return to full activity
ROM	Active and passive knee flexion and extension Hamstring stretching	Continue previous ROM Standing hip flexor stretch	None
Strengthening	Squats range restricted to 0–45 degrees Hip strengthening End of range knee extensions	Continue previous strengthening Increase squat range to 80 degrees Step up/down Straight-ahead lunge	Continue previous strengthening Increase squat range to 90 degrees Lateral lunges
Proprioceptive	Sealed alphabets on ball	Double leg stance BOSU and tilt board Single leg stance whilst brushing teeth	Single leg stance BOSU and tilt board
Restrictions	In water: No diving, tumble turns or breast stroke leg kick On land: No cutting jumping or kicking sports	In water: No diving, gentle breast stroke leg kick On land: No cutting, jumping or kicking sports	None

stroke, due to the awkward angle at which the hips and knee are required to work during the whip kick phase of the stroke. 'Breaststroker's knee' is the term used to describe a chronic medial collateral ligament (MCL) sprain that results from repetitive stress.

Prevention
This injury is usually due to overload, and not a technical error. However, allowing the knees to only separate to hip width during the

stroke will minimize stress on the MCL, and maximize stroke efficiency.

Rehabilitation
The table sets out the symptoms, strengthening exercises and restrictions necessary in knee rehabilitation.

Cramp

Muscle cramps are sudden involuntary muscle

contractions. The most common location is the calf. Muscle cramps can be painful and debilitating, and highly dangerous if they occur when open water swimming. There is a plethora of research surrounding the cause of muscle cramps, although none of it has been conclusive. Currently the weight of this points to neural excitability, although there is some evidence to back up dehydration and specifically low carbohydrate, potassium or sodium levels.

Prevention

Eating a high carbohydrate meal two to three hours before swimming, and maintaining balanced and sufficient fluid and electrolyte stores are beneficial. Fluid containing carbohydrate and electrolytes should be consumed during long races or training sessions (see Chapter 9 for further information on hydration and fuelling).

Treatment

The aim of treatment is to reduce motor neuron and muscle spindle activity. Massage and myofascial trigger-point techniques on the affected tissues have been shown to be beneficial, as have stretching protocols. As muscles work in pairs, restoring normal muscle balance is also of importance. Ice can be used at the time of cramp to decrease pain and speed up the dissipation of the cramp.

CHAPTER 12

FREQUENTLY ASKED QUESTIONS

Over the years I have introduced a large number of people to open water swimming. Some had a great deal of previous swimming experience whilst others were complete novices, but all had one thing in common – lots of questions. In this book I have tried to include, in an orderly fashion, all the information that is necessary for you to get swimming. However, before reaching its conclusion I felt it would be useful to include a short chapter summarizing the information in a short, sharp, question and answer format. In that vein I have summarized the questions that I came across most frequently, along with my answers to them.

Q: How competent do you need to be at swimming in a pool before you attempt an open water event?
A: If you are confident you can complete the distance and have practised swimming in open water, then it is safe for you to compete. Pick an event organized by a company with a good reputation, and one where significant rescue cover is provided. Ideally swim with a friend, and have a friend or two supporting you from dry land. Starting to the side of the pack and towards the back will ensure you have space and are not swum over by everyone else – trust me, this is not a pleasant experience. If you get into trouble, simply roll on to your back and raise your hand. This distress signal will be recognized by

the rescue cover, and they will quickly come to your aid.

Q: I need glasses, so how can I swim?
A: It is possible to swim with contact lenses in under goggles. If you do not like to wear contact lenses, then there are some goggle manufactures who sell their goggles with prescription lenses.

Q: Water pools in my wetsuit around my lower back – does this mean I have the wrong size?
A: I am afraid it is most likely that your suit is too large and you will have to replace it. Wetsuits will give a little as you wear them and so can feel tight the first few times they are worn. As long as they are not restricting your breathing or movement, tighter is better.

Q: During which months is it generally safe to swim in open water in the United Kingdom?
A: In the UK, organized open water swimming venues usually open between mid- and late April, and close from late September to early October.

Q: Is there a temperature of water below which it is not safe to swim?
A: There is no set universal value because everyone has a different tolerance to the cold, but in general the lowest safe temperature is

commonly regarded as 12°C. In water below this temperature it is not safe for the majority of people to swim, nor is it pleasant, even in a wetsuit.

Q: Blue-green algae has been reported at my local open water swimming venue: what are the associated risks or dangers?
A: There have been no reports of long-term illness or death in human beings due to blue-green algae, although the toxins produced by the algae can cause sickness. On the other hand, the algae can be fatal to animals, including dogs and cats. (See Chapter 4 for more detailed information about blue-green algae.)

Q: I am not a strong swimmer, so will I be able to complete an open water swimming event?
A: If you train properly to make sure you are confident that you can complete the set distance, the answer is 'yes'. In your first event I would suggest swimming with a friend – they can check that you are OK, and you can motivate each other both in training and during the event itself.

Q: Are there any open water swimming clubs I can join?
A: Yes. Make a quick internet search and you will find a handful of local clubs. However, if you are simply looking for a like-minded group of people to swim with you will find this at your local open water swimming venue at no extra charge. Just turn up and get chatting.

Q: I am nervous of open water: how can I overcome this fear?
A: In the UK there is nothing to be afraid of in open water, so try to think of it just like a big swimming pool. Start off slowly and in shallow water, and gradually challenge yourself to go a bit further or a bit deeper. Wearing a wetsuit (which you will almost certainly be doing in the UK) does help make you feel protected. Swim with a friend who is patient and knows about your fear, and try to keep as relaxed as possible, and control your breathing to keep yourself calm. (See Chapter 3 for more information.)

Q: I zig-zag a lot when swimming in open water. What advice can you give me other than sighting more frequently?
A: Work on balancing your stroke. If you are struggling to swim in a straight line it is likely to be because you are pulling more with one arm than the other or in a different direction with one arm. Remember that your aim is to make forward progress and so any large side-to-side movements are wasted energy. If possible ask someone to film you from under water. Ask them to take three shots of you: one directly below you as you swim over the top of the camera, one from one side, and one from the other. Then watch these clips back and look for imbalances in your stroke.

Remember that when making changes to your swimming technique, movements that feel large are actually very small. To explain this better, let us consider an example. If on your footage you see that you are entering your left hand across the mid-line of your body, in order to correct this it should feel as if you are entering your hand at around 10 o'clock on a clock face. In reality this will probably mean your hand is entering at 12 o'clock, directly down your body's mid-line as desired.

Q: Swimming in salt water makes me feel sick as it goes down my nose and throat. What can I do to help this?
A: Try swimming with a nose clip, as this will stop the water rushing up your nose. Concen-

trate on keeping your mouth closed whilst swimming, or breathing out continuously whilst your head is under the water. Not only will this stop water flowing into your mouth but it will keep you relaxed. Holding your breath can result in you tensing up. If you are still having problems, simply keep trying. Eventually your body will adjust and stop being so sensitive to the salt water. Have a drink of fresh water close by to rinse out your mouth during and after your swim.

Q: Do I need to wear a swimming hat?
A: For training, no you don't. However, in competition it is advisable for both warmth and visibility, and some races will insist that you wear a specially provided, colour-coded swimming hat. This enables the event staff to track the swimmers involved in their event.

Q: I have a latex allergy, what can I do?
A: Whilst lots of swimming hats contain latex, it is possible to purchase silicon only swimming hats. However, this will not protect you from others who may well wear a latex hat – if, for instance, the official race hat is a latex hat, you may find there is so much latex in the water around the swim pack that it may trigger your allergy. Consequently, if your allergy is quite severe, consider taking long-acting anti-histamine tablets prior to swimming in a public pool or in a stretch of water that others are swimming in. Also make sure that you inform members of staff at the venue at which you are swimming or the event staff. As always, do not swim alone, and make sure the person you swim with knows about your allergy.

Q: I find it hard to breathe to the left. Is it OK to breathe only to my right side?
A: Most swimmers, especially those who take up swimming at a more mature age, find it easier to breathe to one side than the other. This is all right as long as you occasionally carry out a visual check on your other side. If completing a marathon, a 10km race or Channel crossing, it would be advisable to practise breathing to both sides, as breathing purely to one side for such a long duration could result in injury. However, if you are training for a shorter distance it is unlikely to cause you a problem.

Q: I am a triathlete, I come from a running background and am a light runner's build. Swimming is my weakest discipline, how can I improve my swimming without compromising my running speed and endurance?
A: Whilst it is true that having some extra body fat will increase your buoyancy and so improve your swimming efficiency to the detriment of your running, there are some ways you can improve your swimming without affecting your running. Firstly, technique will be very important. Work hard to achieve an efficient technique. A few pointers to start on include: keep your head still; keep rigid in the water (like uncooked spaghetti), not soft and limp (like cooked spaghetti); don't let your legs drop down (work on an efficient leg kick and core strength and stability to conquer this technical faux pas); ensure your timing is correct (body rotation, leg kick, pull); rotate from the hips.

Secondly, if your event is a wetsuit swim your wetsuit will significantly increase your buoyancy and so your build will not be such an issue. Further to this, improve your upper body strength. As a swimmer your arms produce most of the forward movement and so these need to be strong and able to cope with the workload.

Q: How often should I train a week to see improvements in my swimming?
A: I advise three sessions a week. Swim twice

a week and you will maintain your current level, the third session will see you going from strength to strength.

Q: How many kilometres do I need to swim a week to complete a 1,500m swim?

A: How long is a piece of string? It is sensible to complete a session where you swim your race distance, in this case 1,500m. However, this can be with some short breaks, and you most certainly don't need to complete a straight 1,500m each time you get in the water. But covering the distance at least once will give you confidence on the day, and is sensible from the safety aspect. (See the training programme in Chapter 12.)

Q: How long do I need to train up for a 10km race?

A: Once again, how long is a piece of string? This depends on your previous swimming experience and current fitness levels. However, for most people who are fairly good swimmers and have a reasonable fitness level, three months should be enough time to ensure you can safely cover the distance. (See the training programme in Chapter 12.)

Q: I struggled with my training in the month before my event. Should I try to cram things in up to the last minute to make up for this?

A: No, it is better to go into a race slightly 'undercooked' but well rested than to cram in the missed sessions and be tired on the day. Try to put this lack of preparation behind you and draw strength from the training you have completed.

Q: I am competing in an event in a hot climate: what can I do to ensure I stay well hydrated throughout the event?

A: Make sure that when you start the event you are fully hydrated. A few days before, up your water and salt intake. Also consider drinking an electrolyte drink – many of these can be bought over the counter, or you can make your own by combining sugar or fruit juice, water and salt. However, it is possible to over hydrate, and this can result in serious illness and in some severe cases even death, so do be sensible. If your event is likely to last more than an hour, practise taking on fluid and nutrients during training sessions. (How to do this is fully explained in Chapter 9.)

Q: I have entered a Channel crossing: can I wear a wetsuit if it is colder than a certain temperature?

A: Not if you want your crossing to be officially ratified. Recently the authorities have set up categories that allow wetsuits to be worn, but the traditional and most official Channel crossings should be done wearing only a hat, goggles and swimsuit or trunks.

Q: What is the world record for a Dover to Calais crossing?

A: Currently the world record time is 6 hours and 55 minutes. This record is held by the Australian Trent Grimsey and was achieved on 8 September 2012. The Channel varies in width from 34km at its narrowest to 240km at its widest. The first recorded unassisted Channel crossing was made in 1875 by Matthew Webb in 21 hours 45 minutes.

Q: I am a triathlete and struggle to get my wetsuit off quickly in transition – it gets stuck over my ankles. Is it OK to cut the legs off a few inches?

A: Yes, this is fine and actually quite a common thing to do. However, when cutting your suit, remember you can always cut more off, but you can't add more on, so err on the side of caution.

Q: How should I store my wetsuit during the winter months to maximize its longevity?

A: After each use you should wash out your wetsuit with fresh water to remove any salt, oil, lubricant, sweat and so on. Do this with the suit inside out and dry it inside out. Make sure that it is not in direct sunlight whilst drying. Once it is dry, turn it the right way around. Ideally it should be laid out flat to store, at room temperature, and once again not in direct sunlight. Avoid using hangers to hang your suit for a long period of time unless it is a specially designed wetsuit hanger. If you notice a hole or tear in your suit, address this straightaway as with more use it will only get larger. There are kits that you can buy to fix small holes or tears, and with the correct equipment it is fairly easy to do this yourself.

CHAPTER 13

THE FINAL WORD

This book provides you with all the information you need to take on the world of open water swimming. Not everything included will be necessary for everyone to know but hopefully there is something for everyone. I hope that the text has encouraged you to start open water swimming or has enthused you to continue. Be patient with yourself and do not expect progress to occur overnight. Learning and conquering new skills takes time, and in the race of the hare and the tortoise a successful swimmer is always the tortoise. Consistency is key.

Open water swimming can seem rather challenging, but it is in fact an extremely welcoming sport surrounded by a friendly community of active people. With a little time and effort put into training there is an event out there for you, no matter how old, unfit or uncoordinated you are.

I have thoroughly enjoyed writing this book and have learnt a lot along the way. Similarly, I hope that you have enjoyed reading it and that some of the information included has proved useful to you on your path to conquering the open water. Swim safe and enjoy your time with nature.

GLOSSARY

As with all sports, clubs and activities swimming, and especially open water swimming, has its own language. This can seem confusing or act as a barrier stopping you from becoming one of the 'gang'. To make your progress to becoming a 'swimming bilingual' a little easier, I thought it would be useful to outline some of the commonly used open water swimming words and their meanings below. I have aimed for a comprehensive list and thus not all words defined below are mentioned elsewhere in this book, but all come from the language of the swimmer:

abduction   A movement which draws a limb away from the mid-line of the body.

actin and myosin   Actin filaments and myosin are responsible for a range of types of cell movement. In relation to muscles, actin and myosin are responsible for muscular contraction.

aerobic exercise   Exercise at an intensity that results in oxygen being used to create and release energy. This is generally light-to-moderate intensity exercise which can be sustained for an prolonged period of time.

adduction   A movement which draws a limb towards the mid-line of the body

anaerobic exercise   Exercise of a high enough intensity to trigger anaerobic metabolism. This type of exercise cannot be sustained for a long period of time and is used in exercise which rely on speed and power.

asthma   A lung disease whereby the lungs and airwards become inflamed and narrowed. Symptoms are: wheezing; shortness of breath; coughing.

band   A rubber band used in swim training to keep the feet together so that the swimmer cannot kick and has to propel themselves forwards using only their arms.

beach start   Some open water swimming or triathlon events start on a beach with participants lined up on a starting line on the beach. This is referred to as a beach start.

blood glycogen   Glycogen stored in the blood.

blue green alage   Also known as cyanobacteria or cyanophta, this is a phylum of bacteria that carries out photosynthesis to create energy. In the process they go through to create energy, certain toxins are released. These toxins can make human beings sick, but there are no reported cases of them being fatal. However, they can be toxic to some animals including dogs and cats.

BOSU   Stands for both sides up. This is a balance training device which was invented in 1999 by David Weck. The product is an inflated rubber hemisphere attached to a rigid plastic platform.

bronchitis   A condition whereby the tubes to the lungs are swell and produce mucus due to inflammation and irritation.

carbohydrate   Carbon, hydrogen and oxygen combined together to form an organic compound. Fruit, breads, pastas, potatoes, rice, cereals and sweets are all high in carbohydrates.

Channel crossing   In swimming, this refers the swimming from across the English Channel between Dover and Calais.

core   Muscular box with the pelvic floor and hip musculature as the base, diaphragm as the top, abdominals the front and paraspinals and gluteals the back. The muscles within this box form the centre of the functional kinetic chain and act as a corset to help stabilize the spine and pelvis.

Dardanelles   Narrow straight of water north-east of Turkey connecting the Agean Sea to the Sea of Marmara. The Dardanelles is the sight of the first recorded open water swim.

deep water start   This is a common way to start an amateur open water swimming or triathlon event. Two objects create either end of a starting line, usually a boat lined up with a structure on shore. Swimmers must be behind this invisible start line until the command is given to start the race.

deltoids   The muscle that forms the rounded outline of the shoulder.

diaphragm   Made up of skeletal muscle, the thoracic diaphragm (commonly referred to simply as the diaphragm) separates the thorax from the abdomen and contracts to perform respiration.

dolphin diving   The technique used by swimmers in shallow water to propel themselves forwards. Swimmers dive down to the ground and push themselves up and out of the water using their legs and controlling their trajectory with their head and arms.

drafting   The act of swimming close behind or adjacent to another swimmer in order to reduce the amount of energy required to make forward progress.

drag shorts   Baggy shorts worn over a wetsuit or swimming trunks. They create resistance in the water and so make it more difficult to move forwards through the water.

electrolyte   Minerals in your blood that carry an electrical charge. They affect the pH of your blood and consequently affect important processes which are required to be carried out by your body. When you sweat you lose electrolytes; in order to maintain homeostasis and ensure your body can keep functioning as normal these must be replaced.

essential fatty acids   Fatty acids required by the body to maintain normal function which cannot be synthesized by the body and so must be ingested.

etiology   The study of the causes or origin, in a medical sense that is the causes or origin of an injury or disease.

extension   Term used to refer to movement resulting in a body part moving away from the body.

feed station Specified area during an open water swimming event at which food and water is available for consumption. It is normal that the swimmer themselves provides specific food for themselves.

FINA The international governing body of all things in swimming based. Specifically, that includes: swimming; diving; water polo; synchronized swimming and open water swimming.

fins Flippers worn occasionally in swimming training. Often mini fins are used to encourage the swimmer to work leg strength and kicking speed.

flexion The term used to refer to a movement resulting in a limb moving towards the body.

ghost carp Mix of an Ogon and wild koi carp. Identifiable by its silver scales which create its ghostly appearance.

glycogen The main storage form of glucose in human cells.

hand paddles Flat paddles attached to the hand by rubber cords and used to increase upper body strength and improve swimming technique.

Hellespont see Dardanelles.

humerus The bone found in the upper arm.

infraspinatus Thick triangular muscle found in the fossa beneath the spine of the scapular. It is one of the four muscles that make up the rotator cuff. The main function of this muscle is to stabilize the shoulder joint and externally rotate the arm.

intensity The level of effort at which exercise is to be carried out at.

isometric A muscular contraction by which the length of the muscle does not change but the muscle is worked. No movement is created but force is produced.

isotonic A muscular contraction by which the tension in the muscle remains constant but its length changes. Movement is created.

kickboard A float held by swimmers to keep their upper body a float, head out of the water, whilst the legs kick to move the swimmer forwards.

levator scapulae Muscle found at the back of the neck. Its job is to elevate the scapula.

lumbar multifidii A very thin muscle deep in the spine which works to stabilize the joints in the spine at each segmental level.

motor neuron Neurons (nerve cells) located in the central nervous system that project their axons out of the central nervous system and directly or indirectly control muscles.

muscle glycogen Glycogen stored in muscle tissue.

muscle spindle Sensory receptors found in muscle tissue. Their job is to detect changes in muscle length.

nerve synapse A structure that allows a nerve cell to pass a chemical or electrical signal to another cell.

pontoon start Commonly used in elite open water swimming or triathlon events.

The start line is marked on the pontoon and commonly starting boxes are also marked out. One swimmer is permitted in each box and toes must be behind the start line until the command to go is given and the participants then must dive in and start swimming.

protein Biological molecules consisting of at least one chain of amino acids.

pull buoy A float shaped so that it fits comfortably between the upper thighs. It is used to help keep the legs afloat to allow the swimmer to focus on their arms stroke or build strength by isolating the arms.

rash vest Thermal tight-fitting top (can be long or short sleeved) often worn in water sports to provide the wearer with warmth.

refractometer A piece of equipment used to test an individuals hydration level.

reverse zip A zip that does up from bottom to top instead of the conventional top to bottom.

rotator cuff A group of muscles that act to stabilize the shoulder complex.

scapula The shoulder blade. It is a flat, triangular bone that sits on the posterolateral aspect of the rib cage. The scapula connects the clavicle and the humerus.

scapulothoracic motion The movement between the scapula and the thorax (chest wall). This motion is limited by the sternoclavicular and acromioclavicular joints.

Scheurmann's kyphosis A childhood disorder in which the vertebrae grow unevenly with respect to the sagittal plane. This results in kyphosis, or rounding, of the spine.

serratus anterior A muscle located on the lateral aspect of the chest. It originates from the first to ninth or first to either ribs and inserts along the medial border of the scapula. Its job is to pull the scapula forwards on the thorax.

spondylolysis Defect in the pars of the interarticularis of the vertebral arch. Most commonly found in the fifth lumbar vertebrae but can also be present in other lumbar or thoracic vertebrae.

spondylolithesis Displacement of a vertebra or the vertebral column in the anterior or posterior direction in relation to the vertebra below.

sportsmanship The attitude that sport should be involved purely for its own sake and that morals, respect, and fairness should be upheld.

suprasprinatus One of the muscles of the rotator cuff. It is located in the fossa above the spine of the scapula. Its main function is to stabilize the shoulder complex and abduct the arm at the shoulder.

swimskin Similar to a wetsuit but thinner. It provides extra buoyancy and warmth, but not as much as a wetsuit. Swimskins are sometimes allowed to be worn in events where wetsuits are not allowed.

teres minor One of the muscles of the rotator cuff. It runs along the posteriorlateral angle of the scapula. Its primary function is to stabilize the shoulder complex, hold the head of the humerus in the glenoid fossa of the scapula and externally rotate the humerus.

theraband   A stretchy resistance cord used by physiotherapists for rehabilitation or strengthening exercises.

thoracic spine   The middle section of the vertebral column. In human beings it consists of twelve vertebrae.

towelly band   Used to increase the resistance. A towel wrapped around a normal swimming band. Start with a small towel as this makes swimming very challenging.

transverse abdominus   Muscle that runs transversely across the abdomen. It stretches from the pelvis all the way up to the diaphragm. It is made up primarily of tonic, type I muscle fibres and works to stabilize the spine.

trapezius   A large muscle that extends from the occiput (lower part of the skull) to the twelfth thoracic vertebra and the spine of the scapula. As it is such a large muscle, it has three functions. The upper trapezius supports the arm, the middle region retracts the shoulder blade and the lower region medially rotates and depresses the scapulae.

visualization   A technique often used by athletes to aid them in achieving their goals. The athlete envisages themselves in a variety of different sporting situations, they work out and then imagine how they will react to each situation with the end result always being them achieving their goal.

wading   The technique used by swimmers to make fast efficient forward progress in shallow water.

Weill's Disease   Caused by a bacteria in water due to contamination from animal urine, it can affect humans and animals if the contaminated water comes into contact with eyes or unhealed tears in the skin.

FURTHER INFORMATION

2xu
For performance swim and triathlon wear, go to the 2xu UK shop website.
www.2xushop.co.uk

BBC tide timetable
From the weather home page navigate via the 'Coast and Sea' page to the tide timetables section to search for tide times in your area.
www.bbc.co.uk/weather

The Environment Agency
Follow the links through the 'At home and leisure' section to check on the water safety for swimming in your area.
www.environment-agency.gov.uk

FINA
For information on anything and everything aquatic, head to the FINA (Féderation Internationale de Natation) website.
www.fina.org

The Great Swim
The Great Swim is an extremely well-run both beginner- and elite-friendly open water swim series throughout the UK.
www.greatswim.org

Mako
A funky French swimwear and performance wetsuit company. To access the UK shop, head to the following website.
www.makosport.co.uk

Physiotherapy supplies
Elastic bungees, stretch cords and therabands can be purchased from both of the following online stores, along with many other great re- and pre-habilitation tools.
www.physioroom.com
www.physiosupplies.com

Open Water SwimUK
Two open water swimming lakes in the South East of England. The lakes are generally open mid-late April until late September to Early October. There is lifeguard cover, measured laps and both swimming and aquathlon races throughout the season.
www.openwaterswimuk.com

Power Bar UK
Premium sports nutrition
www.powerbar.co.uk

INDEX

A
acclimatization   16–22, 25
   cold water   16–17
   warm water   17
aerobic   34, 52, 55
allergy   21
anaerobic power   53
anaphylactic shock   21
anti-chafing cream   34
anti-fog solution   10

B
balance   29
band
   swim   14
   towelly   15
blue green algae   24, 82
boats   21, 25
body surf   46
breastroker's knee
   MCL sprain   79
buoy   8, 18, 20, 25, 29, 47
   pull   14
buoyancy   25

C
caffeine   53–55
carbohydrate   52, 54
   complex   53
Channel swim   21
competition   33–37
core stability   61–65, 78
cortisol   54
cramp   17, 23, 25, 80
currents   23–28, 35

D
Dardanelles   7
doggy paddle   29
dolphin dive   43
drafting   38–40
   on feet   39
   on hip   40

E
elastic bungee   17, 34
electrolyte   53, 54, 80
   drink   34
endurance   55
environment agency   24
essential fatty acid   52
exit   44

F
fatigue   34, 52
feeding   18
FINA   7, 9–10
fins   14
fish   21, 24
   jelly   21

G
goal   22, 36, 56
goggles   10, 20, 34
   leak   25
   lost   25
glycogen   52

H
hand paddles   14
heat pad   17

Hellespont   7
hydration   17–18, 25, 52–55, 80

I
injury   70–80
iron   55
isotonic
   drink   25

J
jellyfish   (see fish)

K
kayak   (see boat)
kickboard   14
kitbag   34

L
lanolin   17
law   23–25
lightning   23

M
magnesium   25
muscle
   glycogen   (**see** glycogen)
   tonic   66

N
navigable water   25
neoprene hat   34
nerve synapse   36
nutrition   52–55

O
Olympic games   7
overload   70

P
pack swimming   18, 25
paddle board   (see boat)
potassium   25
protein   52
psychology   36

R
rash vest   17, 34
refractometer   17
reservoir   24
reverse zip   11
rotator cuff   17
rough water   20, 31

S
safety   23–25
salt water   20, 31, 46
Schermann's kyphosis   78, 90
serotonin   55
shorts
   drag   14
   neoprene   15
shoulder
   stabilizing complex   8, 66,
      70–78
   swimmer's   70–78
sighting   21, 29–32, 44
silicone ear plugs   17
spondylolisthesis   78
spondylolysis   78
sportsmanship   40
starts   19
   beach   42
   deep water   41
   dive   44
   pontoon   41, 44
stretch cord   (see elastic bungee)
   protocol   66
   static and dynamic   67
swim drills   58
swim snorkel   14
swim suit regulations   9

T
tides   26–28, 35
   rip   23, 27
transisition   29, 46
trespassing   24
triathlon   10, 20, 35
   Olympic distance   54, 57

U
urine 17

V
visualization 32, 36

W
wading 42, 46

warm down 35
warm up 17, 35
warming cream 17
weather 23, 25
weeds 21
Weill's disease 24
wetsuit 10–11, 17, 25, 34
    size 11, 16